IMAGES
of America

ROCK SPRINGS
PARK

The fate of the famed 1927 Dentzel carousel, once housed in the octagonal red-and-green-roofed pavilion at Rock Springs Park, remained a mystery for several decades after it was sold in 1974. (Courtesy of Richard Bowker.)

ON THE COVER: Pleasure seekers pose in the flower gardens of Rock Springs Park's second dance hall, the Casino, in a photograph from around 1906. (Courtesy of Richard Bowker.)

IMAGES
of America

ROCK SPRINGS
PARK

Joseph A. Comm

ARCADIA
PUBLISHING

Published by Arcadia Publishing
Charleston, South Carolina

Library of Congress Control Number: 2009937668

For all general information contact Arcadia Publishing at:
Telephone 843-853-2070
Fax 843-853-0044
E-mail sales@arcadiapublishing.com
For customer service and orders:
Toll-Free 1-888-313-2665

Visit us on the Internet at www.arcadiapublishing.com

To Christian, Caitlyn, Chloe, and Matthew

Rock Springs Park hosted an outdoor wedding in 1908. The wedding party stands on the arched bridge that once spanned the Shoot-the-Chutes ride in the upper park. In the background, park patrons take a thrilling ride on the Figure Eight coaster, while the bride and groom, dressed like two figures atop a wedding cake, exchange their vows. (Courtesy of Richard Bowker.)

CONTENTS

ACKNOWLEDGMENTS

I was only 6 years old when Rock Springs Park closed and 10 when the buildings were razed and the land leveled to make way for Route 30's approach to the Jennings Randolph Bridge. As a child, all I could ever do was stand on the edge of Rock Springs Park and look in, but researching and writing this book has given me the opportunity to finally cross under the wooden supports of the Cyclone roller coaster and enter the world of Rock Springs Park for the first time—a feat that would not have been possible without the help of so many.

Richard Bowker has said many times that Rock Springs Park was his favorite amusement park, and fans are blessed because of it. Unless otherwise noted, all images appearing in this book were graciously provided by Richard Bowker from his vast collection of Rock Springs Park postcards, pictures, and memorabilia. Tish Hand has spent countless hours sharing her personal stories and pictures with me in order to make the Hand years come alive for readers, and it was her daughter, Kassy Hand, whose message to "Write that book" prompted me to begin this journey.

I wish to thank my editor at Arcadia, Amy Perryman, who has been both kind and patient during this process.

Also, thanks go to the following people for sharing their time, stories, images, collections, and/or suggestions: George Allison, Doug Arner and Arner Funeral Chapel, Scott Beck, Rich Brookes, Robin and Chelsea Brown, Donna Chaney-Bell, Wayne Cole, Caitlyn Comm, Christian Comm, Clifford and Margaret Comm, Doug Comm, Judy Comm, James (Del) Cooper, Paul R. Cowey III, Jeff Croushore, Mary Jane Dicky, Clarence O. Durbin, Evelyn Louise Fersch, Robert A. Finley, Fred Fischer, Jim Futrell, Joe Geiger, William and Donna Gray, Sayre W. Graham Sr., Kassy Hand, Tish Hand, Betty Hardman and Fox Nursing Home, Charles J. Jacques Jr., Edith and Tom Jagger, Mary Lawrence, William Linkenheimer, Richard Z. Macdonald, Bill Mackall, Jen Matsick, Michael D. McElwain, Dean McKinney, Dan Omlor, David Rhoades, Barbara Scott, Dr. Mike West, and Mary Ann Wright.

There is a select group of people who have prepared the way for this book through their research, writing, and enthusiasm for Rock Springs Park. Specifically I wish to thank Roy C. Cashdollar, Alvin Fineman, George Hines, Ira Sayre, Constance Watters Miles, Susan Weaver, and the volunteers of the Memory Lane Group of Chester and the Tri-State Genealogical and Historical Society.

Finally, to my wife, Linda, thank you for your love and support, not just in this project, but in everything.

INTRODUCTION

Rock Springs Park was an amusement park located in the Upper Ohio River Valley town of Chester, West Virginia. Chester, situated at the extreme northern limit of Hancock County, lies directly across the Ohio River from East Liverpool. The area is best known for its iconic World's Largest Teapot and pottery industry, including Homer Laughlin China Company with its world-renowned Fiesta Dinnerware.

A onetime stop along the Catawba Trail, the area attracted Native Americans and early settlers with its bubbling mineral springs and abundance of wild game. It is widely believed that George Washington drank from Rock Springs when he and his party, including the Native Americans Half King, Pheasant, and White Feather, camped near the entrance to the park on the night of October 21st, 1770.

The site of the springs was first used for picnics in 1857; its wondrous scenic setting was advertised as the perfect getaway for church outings and other civic affairs. In the early 1880s, wharf master Patsy Kernan leased the Marks Farm, including Rock Springs Park, and arranged for the ferryboat *Ollie Neville* to carry pleasure seekers to his scenic wonderland.

East Liverpool attorney James (J. E.) McDonald acquired 170 acres of the Marks estate in 1890 with a plan to commercialize the spring grove by building a local amusement park in conjunction with a new bridge project and streetcar line. Despite several setbacks, work on the bridge and park began in 1895. The 1,466-foot bridge was completed in just over a year, and the trolley had its first run on May 26, 1897. Three days later, on Memorial Day 1897, Rock Springs Park had its official opening, where, according to author and Chester historian Roy C. Cashdollar, "more than 5,000 jammed the dance pavilion, café, dining hall, shooting gallery, bowling alleys, walked the shady paths, or watched a ballgame."

"Over the next 10 years," wrote Susan Weaver in a 1985 edition of *Goldenseal Magazine*, "through the leadership and financial support of men such as McDonald and his successor, Charles (C. A.) Smith, Rock Springs Park grew to become the showcase of the area." It offered many popular attractions, such as swimming, boating, picnic grounds, promenade walks, and amusement rides—including the merry-go-round, Shoot-the-Chutes, Old Mill, and Smith's crown jewel, the World's Greatest Scenic Railway. The park flourished until 1912, when the Central Passenger Association "rescinded all Pennsylvania Railroad excursion business," and a series of devastating fires forced park management to proclaim it the poorest season the park had ever seen.

Charles (C. C.) Macdonald and wife, Grace, owners of Summit Park in Akron, Ohio, purchased Rock Springs Park in 1926. Macdonald pledged, according to Weaver, "to bring the park back in popularity and in improvements to the days when it was a popular playground and outing spot in West Virginia." Part of Macdonald's plan to modernize the park included replacing the scenic railway with a $25,000, state-of-the-art wooden roller coaster, adding a small zoo, and upgrading the dance pavilion, which he christened "Virginia Gardens" in honor of his 18-year-old daughter. For two seasons, the park saw record attendance and profits, leading former owner C. A. Smith to comment that the crowds were the largest he had ever seen within the gates of the park.

With the onset of the Depression, Macdonald needed to diversify in order to keep Rock Springs Park going. To that end, he moved his family to Ligonier, Pennsylvania, in 1931 to become partner to Richard B. Mellon and part owner of Idlewild Park. Grace Macdonald went back and forth between Rock Springs and Idlewild for four years until turning the entire operation of Rock Springs Park over to her newly wedded daughter, Virginia, and son-in-law, Robert L. Hand, in 1935. The Hands would spend the next 35 years in Rock Springs Park, raising two sons and sustaining a modest but profitable existence until the park was purchased, rides and all, by the State of West Virginia in 1974.

Peering down the chain-lift hill of the Shoot-the-Chutes ride, this panoramic postcard clearly illustrates the development of industrialization and entertainment at the dawn of the 20th century. In the foreground is Rock Springs Park, the tri-state area's premier panhandle playground, and rising in the background is the black smoke of a tin mill (left) and a series of cone-shaped pottery kilns (right).

One

THE ALLURE OF

ROCK SPRINGS

EARLIEST HISTORY–1889

It is difficult to pinpoint exactly what draws people to an amusement park that has been gone for nearly 40 years. Perhaps it is the same force that attracted the early Panhandle Archaic Indians to the Upper Ohio Valley well over 4,000 years ago. To the native people, the shaded grove of trees along Marks Run was a sacred hunting ground. Not far from the park, at the northernmost bend of the Ohio River, a great treaty was made between six powerful American Indian nations. This council met at a large flat rock on the beach, confirming their peace agreement by carving tribal symbols on the rock face. Rock Springs Park owner C. A. Smith offered a 15-minute sightseeing tour to the stone drawings in 1910, explaining that they would soon be "forever covered by the rising waters of the Ohio River"—a direct result of the completion of Dam No. 8.

Before the land was used for picnics and amusements, George Washington took an interest in the area. He travelled through this region on more than one occasion, camping on western lands. In July 1758, his journal recalls Babb's Island directly across from Rock Springs Park, where to lighten his load and flee Native Americans he buried a barrel of crackers. Then in October 1770, Washington reportedly camped near the entrance to Rock Springs Park and drank from its refreshing mineral spring waters.

Rock Springs Park marks its beginning in 1857, when the land known as Rock Springs Grove was first donated for church picnics. Local wharfmaster Patsy Kernan leased the property and arranged for the ferryboat *Ollie Neville* to carry picnickers across the Ohio River to what was then called "the southside" in Virginia. For the first time, visitors could spend the day enjoying the simple pleasures of hiking trails, picnic shelters, and a 16-foot dancing platform. "Over the next several years," wrote Susan Weaver, "[Kernan] continued to improve the grounds by adding a lunchroom, baseball diamond, roller rink, and merry-go-round. In 1893, Patsy relinquished his management of the resort and was succeeded by L. J. McGhie, who operated the park with little change for the next three years." By 1897, a new bridge and streetcar were added, and within just a few years, Rock Springs Park was transformed into a full-fledged trolley park.

9

This early view of Marks Run displays the natural beauty of the park prior to commercial development.

Two men sit on the largest boulder found on the hillside near Rock Springs. A map of the area dated 1871 shows no town or village of Chester, but a label identifies the springs and "Rock Springs Farm."

In the photograph above, rows of ceramic cups line a shelf above the spring, and a primitive wooden water cooler is fitted with faucets. In the mid-19th century, the Upper Ohio Valley was described as a series of potters' fields, not for the biblical burial place but because of the rich crockery-making industry.

Transportation to Rock Springs in the early years was difficult. When the river was low, people drove across by wagon. Evelyn Fersch of East Liverpool recalled her mother's tale of traveling to the park from New Cumberland in the 1890s by horse and buggy: "My grandmother would pack the children's favorite cheese sandwiches in a picnic basket. To pass the time they would sing hymns along the way. My uncle, who was just a small boy at the time, got the lyrics mixed up and sang, 'We shall come rejoicing, bringing in the cheese [instead of sheaves].' " In the photograph above, weary travelers take a refreshing drink from a spring located in the lower level of the park. The tree behind them is covered with the carved initials of visitors past.

This *c.* 1889 photograph labeled "Family Reunion and Wedding at Rock Springs Park" is from the collection of Ira Sayre. For many years after the park closed, Sayre enjoyed sharing his slide show presentation of photographs and postcards of the park with area civic groups. "I took some pictures before it was entirely defunct, and then started to collect pictures from some of the older photographers," Sayre said in an article appearing in the *Evening Review*, May 7, 1994. "The older age groups remember the park, and like reliving those memories." (Courtesy of Rich Brookes.)

The Ollie Neville awaits additional passengers on the banks of the Ohio River along the Broadway wharf in East Liverpool. The 93-foot stern-wheel steamer provided service to the park until 1897, when it was made obsolete by the new bridge and streetcar line. On the opposite shore, only a few homes are visible along the broad cape-like headland of Chester. The *Ollie Neville* ended its run working trade routes in Lake Erie, where it sank off the banks of Ripley, New York, in 1905. It is now listed among hundreds of non-diveable shipwrecks at the bottom of the lake. (From the Collection of the Public Library of Cincinnati and Hamilton County.)

Two

J. E. McDonald Years
1890–1899

James (J. E.) McDonald was an East Liverpool attorney with an eye for real estate. In 1890, he purchased 170 acres of the A. E. Marks Estate for $17,000 with the notion that the flat headlands of the Southside of East Liverpool would make for an ideal expansion to the hilly pottery town. The Marks Farm included 11 acres of Rock Springs Park, managed at that time by L. J. McGhie. In 1893, McDonald announced plans for the erection of a new bridge between the Southside and East Liverpool. His plan included a trolley line and the expansion of the humble picnic grove into a full-fledged amusement park. It took three years to obtain enough investors to undertake the $250,000 construction project, due in large part to the national financial panic of 1893. When work on the bridge and the new park began in 1896, there were still fewer homes along an unpaved Carolina Avenue in what McDonald and others would later call "Chester."

Often there is confusion about two of the original owners of Rock Springs Park due to the fact that they had similar-sounding names. While J. E. McDonald was overseeing the excavation for his bridge piers in June 1896, young future owner Charles (C. C.) Macdonald was just entering the park world in Mount Vernon, Ohio, where he operated a popcorn and peanut concession. A little over a year later, J. E. McDonald watched the first trolley of the Chester and East Liverpool Street Railway Company cross his new bridge and travel to the end of the line. McDonald was delighted when thousands of people attended Rock Springs' official opening on Memorial Day; meanwhile, a young C. C. Macdonald pulled taffy for D. S. Humphrey, owner of Euclid Beach Park in Cleveland. J. E. McDonald is sometimes credited with giving Chester its name by popularizing its use in many of his business advertisements, but there can be no doubt that he is the man who helped transform Rock Springs Park from "Nature's Beauty Spot" to the "Showcase of the East."

A beautiful young woman poses inside a hollow tree, demonstrating that visitors to J. E. McDonald's new trolley park would have been dressed in their Sunday best. The parasol, high, boned collar, and flowing silhouette indicate this photograph was taken during the period described by historians as "The Last Age of Elegance."

On May 26, 1897, the first electric trolley of the Chester and East Liverpool Street Railway Company crossed the new Chester Bridge and traveled to Rock Springs Park. Initially there was only one car in operation on the new line. At that time, conductor James McKinnon made a round-trip each hour.

Shown here festooned in bunting, the original main pavilion, constructed in 1897 by J. E. McDonald, overlooks the trolley station on Carolina Avenue. It was no mere coincidence that the Chester trolley line ended at the entrance to the park. Trolley companies around the country started building amusement parks at the end of their lines to build ridership and increase profits on weekends.

This vintage photograph offers a side view of the main pavilion. Note the beautiful arch motif used throughout the wooden structure. The only building remaining from this early period when the park closed in 1970 was the Ladies Rest House. (Courtesy of Arner Funeral Chapel.)

In this early view of the midway, the large building at left displays a patriotic eagle. A sign on the small building to the right reads, "Tintype Gallery," and a ticket booth with a small step stool for pint-sized patrons sits adjacent to a loading station. Above it, a portion of the Figure Eight roller coaster can be seen. The original dance hall is visible at the end of the midway, and the roof of the park's first carousel pavilion is in the foreground at right.

These two rare photographs show the first carousel pavilion from two different perspectives. An 1897 merry-go-round replaces one that had been operated by Patsy Kernan. Unlike the later Dentzel model, this carousel was of the menagerie style, meaning it featured other animals besides horses. A giraffe is clearly visible at center. In 1906, the menagerie carousel was sold and sent to Mexico, replaced by a new Coney Island model.

These two photographs illustrate the early landscape efforts of J. E. McDonald. Above, young trees take root on the hillside next to the Figure Eight coaster and upper mall area. In the background sits the original dance hall, the Ohio River, and the hills of East Liverpool. Below is a rare glimpse of the midway before the octagonal carousel pavilion was constructed. The small sign near the two figures at right warns visitors to keep off the grass.

From the start, professional gardeners and landscape artists enhanced the natural beauty of Rock Springs Park with formal gardens. Above, sedate young ladies dressed in high fashion point to an attractive flower garden on the lawn of the first dance hall. Their own feathered hats and layered bodices seem to mirror the dense foliage they admire.

LADIES' REST HOUSE, ROCK SPRINGS PARK, CHESTER, W. VA.

This postcard shows the Ladies Rest House as it looked in the 1890s. In a later colorized postcard of the same view, an artist has removed the pole at center. Often postcard artists would romanticize images by removing all undesirable features, such as telephone poles, junkyards, background clutter, and sometimes even cars and people by painting or air-brushing.

This one-of-a-kind rotating fountain would have presented a wonderful and cooling display in the heat of the day, much like the high-pressure cool mist sprays used in amusement parks today. The curtain spray created by the conduit frame along with the base lights and dozens of reflecting mirrors would have made this a spectacular sight at night for ladies and their escorts taking a romantic stroll.

Three

C. A. SMITH YEARS
1900–1925

Charles (C. A.) Smith, "one of the Upper Ohio Valley's most successful and colorful sons" according to the Lou Holtz Upper Ohio Valley Hall of Fame, was only 33 years old when his Steubenville, East Liverpool, and Beaver Valley Traction Company purchased Rock Springs Park in 1900. The last of eight children, Smith began his career at the age of 17 in the gas and oil business, first as a water boy and then laying pipe. He eventually became owner of the Ohio Valley Gas Company until selling off the business in 1898. Smith continued to expand his business interests: in 1900, he became a major stockholder in his brother John's Taylor, Smith, and Taylor (TS&T) pottery plant in Chester and later purchased the Chester Bridge from the then-bankrupt East Liverpool Bridge Company.

C. A. Smith spent hundreds of thousands of dollars updating and expanding the park. Smith added such attractions as the Coney Island merry-go-round and pavilion, the Casino dance hall, the summer theater, the Old Mill, and the World's Greatest Scenic Railway. Smith also added a grandstand to the ball field and constructed boating and bathhouse facilities in 1904, including a 70-foot-by-170-foot swimming pool and a $50,000 three-and-a-half-acre lake.

Smith's first seven years as owner were successful due in large part to his upgrades, as well as the extension of the Kenilworth line into Chester. Train and steamboat excursion trips brought large group outings from Pittsburgh and Wheeling. Attendance only began to decline when a ruling in 1912 by the Central Passenger Association turned the tide. Owners like C. A. Smith fought the decision to end reduced-rate excursion tickets, but in July 1913, Susan Weaver explained, "the Interstate Commerce Commission ruled against picnickers." Woes continued in 1914 as the first of several devastating fires destroyed the Casino dance hall, followed by a second fire in 1915 that destroyed the Old Mill. When a single fire in 1917 consumed the summer theater, the bathhouse, and the icehouse, only the bathhouse was rebuilt, leaving the lower entrance gate section of Rock Springs Park empty. In the upper park, a third dance hall was constructed in 1915, but the slow decline continued until just after the 1925 season ended and a new owner took over the park.

Employees of East Liverpool Traction and Light, including owner C. A. Smith (back row, 6th from left), take a break from their duties to pose for a company photograph. The conductor is flanked by a crew of ticket takers, each sporting coin changers hanging from their belts. Electric trolley cars provided regular and comfortable transport to and from Rock Springs Park from its official opening on May 30, 1897, until 1934, when C. A. Smith converted to bus transport.

The Entrance at Rock Springs Park.

Over the course of nearly a century, the entrance to Rock Springs Park changed several times. When the original main pavilion and entrance were razed in 1905, a new trolley station and lower park entrance were added just above Marks Run, shown here in 1908.

C. A. Smith's home still stands on the terraced hillside above the junction of State Route 2 and old U.S. Route 30 in Chester. Roy C. Cashdollar wrote of this location, "In the spring of 1905, Mr. Smith moved into his new home on Pyramus Avenue, overlooking Rock Springs Park. In the 1930s, he had an addition built." Today the Smith House overlooks the World's Largest Teapot, pictured below. The Chester icon was moved to its present location adjacent to the Jennings Randolph Bridge in 1990 and completely renovated thanks to the efforts of then-mayor Roy C. Cashdollar and retired general contractor Sayre W. Graham Sr. (Below courtesy of Christian Comm.)

The first passenger trains began to arrive in Chester in 1900 on a branch of the Pennsylvania Railroad from Kenilworth. These excursion trains quickly tripled attendance at the park. A schedule from 1910 lists travelers arriving from as far away as Irwin and Trafford, Pennsylvania, a distance of well over 60 miles one way. The train from Irwin departed at 7:45 a.m. at a cost of $1.55 round-trip for one adult, and the last train left Rock Springs Park at 7:30 p.m. Many Chester youths took advantage of these early departure times, receiving free tickets from excursionists making a hasty retreat to their train or boat.

Arriving at Rock Springs Park.

A newspaper account entitled "Grand Excursion" from the June 20, 1900, *Oakdale Times* describes a colorful train ride from Pennsylvania. "The trip was through a country varied in its scenery and interests. The wheat fields in their skimming beauty of sunshine and shadow changing to the golden color of ripening grain. We passed through the Ohio Valley where tile and fire brick is the only industry. This valley seems to be the home of the fruit trees, for acres and acres of hillsides are covered with apple and pear trees. Another interesting industry is the pottery works. One can see the process from the clay until dishes of the coarsest to the very finest are ready for the table. The town of Chester is new, so new that many of the large buildings have not been painted. The park is new, but in a few years it will rival Idlewild [an amusement park in Ligonier, Pennsylvania]."

Area businesses and local school districts booked large group excursions to Rock Springs Park. Residents in East Liverpool and Chester still remember the excitement of finding park tickets in their final report card envelopes, while employees of the Westinghouse Air Brake Company found comic illustrations, such as these, in their 1910 company picnic brochures. Each illustration depicts employees speeding to the park in Rube Goldberg–style racers. Below, a passenger is sacrificed to lighten the load of a dirigible, ensuring a faster trip for the lucky crew remaining.

An American flag flew high above the ornate double gates and gleaming white arches of the lower park entrance. From here, visitors could walk straight ahead and wait in line for the Old Mill ride or continue on the main promenade to other attractions found in the lower park, including the famous mineral springs, lake, bathing pavilion, and pool. To the right was a path to the upper park and new casino.

Rock Springs Park, W. Va. At the Entrance.

This vintage postcard shows well-dressed park visitors mingling just inside the lower entrance. From his hillside home, C. A. Smith would have had an unobstructed view of the thousands of animated men, women, and children disembarking from trains, trolleys and boats for a day of fun at the park.

26

Lilly Pond and Fountain
Rock Springs Park, Chester W.Va.

Two postcards depict the many lily ponds and fountains found throughout the park. Each one was unique, but all were constructed stone by stone from local river rock. Below, a man appears to be contemplating a wish before tossing a coin into one such fountain, thick with floating water lilies. The shade of the trees and cool spray of the fountain would have been welcome respite from the clamor and excitement of the amusements in the upper park.

The Lily Fountain, Rock Springs.

Main Promenade Walk,
Rock Springs Park, Chester, West Va.

The Main Promenade Walk lay just inside the lower entrance to Rock Springs Park. To the left is the Old Mill, or "Aquarama." The Old Mill was a pleasure canal built in 1903. A large paddle wheel was used to maintain a current in the canal, and passengers traveled by boat in a maze of water channels 6 feet wide and over 1,500 feet long. Special rooms along the way displayed historical scenes against canvas backdrops. A similar ride in nearby Kennywood Park in Pittsburgh, Pennsylvania, is still in operation and in vintage postcard pictures appears much the same as the Old Mill in Rock Springs. (Below courtesy of Christian Comm.)

Ye Olde Mill, Rock Springs Park
Chester W. Va. near E. Liverpool Ohio

Decoration Day

CELEBRATION!

--AT--

ROCK SPRINGS PARK

MONDAY, MAY 31st, 1915

Better Than Ever - - - New Dancing Pavillion
18,000 Square feet of Dancing Service

Dancing, Afternoon and Evening
FIRST CLASS ORCHESTRA

Boating, Bathing and all Amusement
Features in Operation

Special Service on all Trolley Lines

Annual School Picnic of East Liverpool, Wellsville, Newell and
and Chester, SATURDAY, JUNE 5TH, 1915

SPEND DECORATION DAY AT THE PARK, CHESTER W. VA.

Flyers like this one featuring the Dance Pavilion appeared locally in storefronts and shop windows. The "New Dancing Pavillion" was built to replace the Casino dance hall after it was destroyed by fire. Visitors spent the day boating on the lake, cooling off in the pool, riding rides, playing penny arcade games, and being entertained in the twilight hours by a "First Class Orchestra." Eerily, the school picnic day advertised at the bottom of the poster is the very one during which four schoolchildren perished in a tragic accident at the Old Mill. (Courtesy of Joe Geiger of West Virginia Archives and History.)

The Old Mill was one of the most popular attractions at Rock Springs Park until it was destroyed by a disastrous fire on June 5, 1915. The fire claimed the lives of four children visiting the park during an annual school picnic. Albert Rayner (12) of Chester and Eva Dales (14) and Glenna Stout (17), both of Newell, died within hours of the fire from burns and shock. Hyacinth Mackey (15) of Newell died two weeks later. Dr. G. W. Wentz of Chester General Hospital, who had been at her side, stated that "the general condition of the girl was improved but her heart failed at the last." The cause of the fire was never determined, but owner C. A. Smith theorized that it was caused by a lighted cigarette dropped in the entrance.

Spectators who were there when the fire started stated that they believed the dynamo (generator) caused the blaze. The dynamo and chain drive are clearly visible in the photograph above. The Old Mill was never rebuilt and was the only amusement ride ever to run in the lower level of Rock Springs Park. Several other fires plagued the Smith years at Rock Springs Park but none with such devastating results as that of the Old Mill fire. (Courtesy of Arner Funeral Chapel.)

On the Rocks — Rock Springs.

About 50 yards beyond the lower entrance to Rock Springs, several generations of one family take a relaxing break "on the rocks." These enormous boulders would have been exposed after millions of years of erosion, the same process that unearthed the familiar rock face of Rock Springs and carved out the entire Upper Ohio Valley region.

This rare photograph taken prior to 1915 shows the lower park in winter. The wooden steps lead to the famous Rock Springs and a refreshment and postcard stand (bottom left). In the upper left background, the Old Mill is visible through the cold morning fog and trees with its "Aquarama" sign above the entrance. Other structures along the two paths of the lower park at this time were the summer theater, ice house, and picnic pavilions. (Courtesy of the Memory Lane Collection.)

The Famous Rock Spring, Rock Springs Park, Chester. W. Va.

These "his and hers" postcards from the C. A. Smith era show perhaps the most famous views of Rock Springs Park. A promotional brochure from the period describes the water of Rock Springs as "clear, cold, sparkling, absolutely pure and has been running for ages."

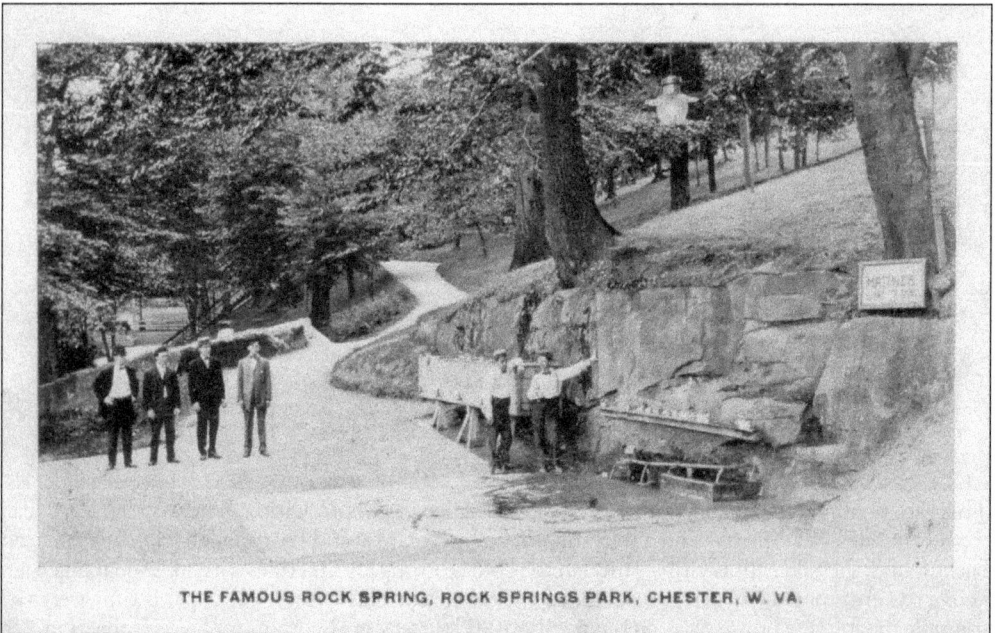

THE FAMOUS ROCK SPRING, ROCK SPRINGS PARK, CHESTER, W. VA.

DINNER TIME, ROCK SPRINGS PARK, CHESTER, W. VA.

A 1910 advertisement for the steamer *St. Paul* of Pittsburgh offers cafeteria lunch and refreshments on board and suggests to travelers that it is "Not necessary to pack your basket lunch for the park unless you prefer." Based on these postcards, park guests apparently preferred to save their money and pack their meals. Hundreds could be seated in picnic pavilions such as these found midway along the main promenade of the lower park.

Rock Springs Park, W. Va. Dining Pavilion.

Audience members stream from the summer theater after viewing an afternoon matinee. Constructed in 1903, the theater was located in the flat area of the lower park across from the picnic pavilions. Roy C. Cashdollar wrote, "The theater used many touring companies that played on the New York stages. Each season several musical comedies and minstrels were presented. The entertainers would live at various rooming houses in the city. Cottages were also built for visiting entertainers to use. The theater was open six months out of the year and for an admission fee of 20¢ one could see a first-class production." (Courtesy of the Memory Lane Collection.)

HOW DO YOU DO
"THE TWO ADMIRALS," AT ROCK SPRINGS THEATRE, JULY 24.

An advertising postcard above for *The Two Generals* shows a couple of comedic actors tipping their hats to two young ladies. The back of the postcard reads, "Adams and Guhl, Musical Comedy Co. at Rock Springs Theater, Twice Daily Commencing Monday, July 24th. 20 People, Mostly Girls." In 1918, the *New York Clipper Vaudeville News and Reviews* said of Adams and Guhl, "They scored a laughing hit. Their talk is funny and well put over. The bits of business are well handled and got many laughs."

Rock Springs Park, W. Va. Interior, Summer Theatre.

Another picture postcard shows an interior view of the summer theater. Packed houses enjoyed plays, recitals, concerts, and minstrels. The stage is shown with a series of scenic backdrops. Trading companies now sell vintage backdrops such as these for as much as $2,000, but unfortunately, fire consumed the summer theater and its contents in 1917.

Rock Springs Park. West Va., Theatre.

BUILDING ROCK SPRING'S SWIMMING POOL Chester, W.V.

The verandas of the bathhouse offered a view of the lake, where long lines formed to take an afternoon sail. Boaters could row around Bower Island in the freshwater spring lake in the morning, then change into bathing suits and cool off in the swimming pool, seen here under construction in 1904. In 1916, the second balcony of the bathhouse collapsed, injuring spectators who were watching a drowning woman being rescued from the pool.

Guests step from the veranda to the viewing platform to watch the swimmers frolic in the water below. Once wet, bathers' wool swimsuits made swimming a bit of a challenge by adding considerable weight to the body.

A sign painted on the back wall of the viewing platform seen in early postcard pictures warned, "Tobacco and Profanity Strictly Forbidden," an early effort to maintain a family atmosphere at the park. Pictured in 1918 are Ola and Kathryn Allison of Chester (back row right) in this group of park guests. The Allison family dates back to the 1850s in Chester, when only nine families owned farmland in the area. By 1921, a report was made by the West Virginia State Board of Health regarding the outdoor pool owned by Smith. It recommended the installation of a chlorinator and recirculating pump and filter, stating that they were necessary "in order that a continuous supply of safe water may be supplied to bathers. This is very important, particularly since many excursions from Ohio and Pennsylvania are made to this park and many of the excursionists use the pool. Thus the spread of disease over a wide area is possible." (Courtesy of George Allison.)

The subsequent installation of a chlorinator and pump is evidenced in a later brochure, which reads, "Crystal Pool filled with clean, clear, chlorinated spring water for bathing. This water is constantly being aerated, and a daily analysis of the water is taken and posted at the entrance for the benefit of the patrons." Near the bathhouse, swimmers could wade into the icy spring-fed waters of the crystal pool. Here, at the opposite end, a swimmer dives headfirst into 12 feet of water.

Smith constructed Rock Springs Park's 3.5-acre lake in 1900. The lake was located at the southern end of the lower park and was bordered on the east by the Lincoln Highway, now Route 30. Today the new highway winds through Chester precisely over the area where the lake once existed. The sign on the island reads, "All Boats Must Keep to the Right." (Courtesy of the Memory Lane Collection.)

On a hot sunny day in 1918, visitors choose a refreshing swim in the pool over a ride in the rowboats, while still others opt for a cool drink on the veranda of the bathhouse at left.

A wooden bridge leads to the "Rustic House" above Spring Lake Lagoon on a steep hillside. In 1906, the tracks of the World's Greatest Scenic Railway, a gravity-operated ride, were laid along the natural curve at the top of this hill. The railway opened the following year on May 24, 1907.

A very popular 1915 postcard view of Bower Island and the lake at Rock Springs Park shows three women standing on a hiking trail near the island. In winter, the bathhouse was heated, and the lake was used for ice-skating. Blocks of ice were also cut from the lake and delivered by a long chute to an icehouse in the lower park. The ice was packed in hay and sawdust and used to make frozen treats like ice cream and sorbet desserts for thousands of park patrons in the sweltering hot days of summer. (Courtesy of Christian Comm.)

An advertisement for the park describes the paths and bridges of Rock Springs Park as "radiating in every direction." These trails "take the visitor to tumbling mountain streams and forest glades, and open spaces, away from the noise of the city and amusements." Above, an early postcard shows a couple pausing at Lover's Lane before continuing along a path which led "to sylvan bowers, and delightful nooks for lover's retreats," according to the *Oakdale Times*. Below is a bridge that spanned the Main Promenade of the lower park.

If peace and serenity could be found in the beauty of the lower park and its natural features, then those seeking the noise and excitement of amusements would have made their way to the upper park, shown here in a panoramic postcard from 1911. From left to right are the baseball diamond, the World's Greatest Scenic Railway, the Shoot-the-Chutes pool, the Casino dance hall and the Figure Eight. (Courtesy of Christian Comm.)

Rock Springs Park grew rapidly under the ownership of C. A. Smith. Crowds like the ones seen here jamming the midway flocked to the park because of the many featured attractions added between 1900 and 1912. The banner in the background reads, "Chicken and Waffle Dinners 50¢," a Pennsylvania Dutch dish consisting of a plain waffle with pulled, stewed chicken on top, covered in gravy. (Courtesy of the Memory Lane Collection.)

41

The baseball diamond at Rock Springs Park was added in 1900 and hosted many famous athletes, like George "Scoops" Carey from the Ohio and Pennsylvania Baseball League. The "O&P" was an area league that began in 1905. Over the course of several years, the league included teams from East Liverpool, Canton, Massillon, Mount Vernon, Newark, Akron, Lancaster, Mansfield, Youngstown, and Zanesville in Ohio, and Sharon, Erie, Homestead, New Castle and Braddock in Pennsylvania. (Courtesy of the Memory Lane Collection.)

The posters displayed on this storefront read, "Patriotic Day, Rock Springs Park. Come Spend the Day! Base Ball [sic] Game 2:30 p.m. E. Liverpool Pirates vs. Steubenville, All amusements will be in operation."

In an unnerving twist on the pony ride, children ride a bull restrained only by a nose ring and slight section of chain link. Park owner C. A. Smith began raising prized Hereford cattle in 1917 at his Hillcrest Farm. In the last 10 years of his life, Smith won best head at international livestock competitions in Chicago, Baltimore, and Kansas City with his grand champion bulls. According to Chester historian Roy C. Cashdollar, "His main breeding bull—HC Larry Domino XII—sold for $105,000 in 1951."

SCENIC RAILWAY, ROCK SPRINGS PARK, CHESTER, W. VA.

In 1906, alongside the baseball stadium, Smith built the World's Greatest Scenic Railway, a gravity-operated train that coasted for a mile through the picturesque setting. Although the attraction cost $30,000 to build, Cashdollar notes in his History of Chester: The Gateway to the West that "the railway paid for itself in its first year of operation at 5¢ a ride." His claim suggests at least 600,000 paying customers rode this precursor to today's wooden and steel coasters in one season.

A vintage photograph reveals that the scenic railway cars were adorned with carved dragon heads connected by a hand bar. A brakeman stands in the back and would have controlled the speed of the car for the length of the trip. Safety rules today would not permit the little girl in front to sit on the car and dangle her feet above the tracks despite the fact that it makes a delightful picture.

This 1907 photograph shows a train of cars descending along the spiral track of the World's Greatest Scenic Railway before carrying passengers on their mile-long tour of Rock Springs Park. The ride continued to be a featured attraction at Rock Springs Park until 1926. (Courtesy of the Memory Lane Collection.)

Ladies pose on a fallen tree that has warped into a natural arched bridge below the tracks of the World's Greatest Scenic Railway. This section of the ride was located directly above the crystal spring lake.

In 1921, the scenic railway was redesigned and billed as a roller coaster. In 1927, the Cyclone roller coaster took its place and its title. Above, the slow-moving gravity ride appears to have been stopped to allow riders and spectators to pose for a photograph. (Courtesy of the Memory Lane Collection.)

Electric lines connect to light poles extending in a repeated series above the track of the World's Greatest Scenic Railway. A ride at night through the wooded hillside of the upper park would have added some thrill of excitement to this mostly tame pleasure ride.

Unlike today's modern roller coasters, scenic railways were relatively slow moving and designed for sightseeing. Here a train of cars carries passengers around the final turn before returning to the upper level of the three-story station house.

Merry Go Round, Rock Springs.

The golden age of the American carousel paralleled that of the trolley companies, and Rock Springs Park was no exception. In 1906, C. A. Smith contracted the Finley Brothers Construction Company of Chester to build an octagonal carousel pavilion to house a carousel manufactured in Coney Island, New York. With a diameter of 90 feet and standing 65 feet tall at its peak, the centrally located building remained an icon of Rock Springs Park until 1974, when the park was stripped of all buildings in the name of progress.

This rare broken-edged tintype photograph reveals that the carousel pavilion from the McDonald era remained in the midway of the upper park and was converted into a formal dining space. Covered tables and wooden chairs surround a central serving counter, signs at front advertise dinner, and a cashier stands at the only exit to the fenced-in pavilion. The larger sign across the midway advertises the "fast food" of the times: "Hot Weiners and Hamburgers 5¢."

The carousel waiting platform and mall were filled with spectators when "free-acts" such as these acrobats performed twice daily. Lyricists of the day warned of these daring young men. In the background, Leap the Dips (an original side friction roller coaster built by the E. Joy Morris Company of Philadelphia) replaces the park's first coaster, the Figure Eight. Leap the Dips was built in 1906 and remained in the park until 1921. (Courtesy of the Memory Lane Collection.)

Next to Leap the Dips (left) was the towering Shoot-the-Chutes ride (center). This water thrill ride consisted of a flat-bottomed boat that slid down a 50-foot flume into a man-made lagoon in seven seconds. Rock Springs Park circulated 12 boats in a continuous run. Shoot-the-Chutes rides were the centerpiece of Luna Parks, a design used today in Lost Kennywood in Pittsburgh and its ride the Pittsburg [sic] Plunge. (Courtesy of the Memory Lane Collection.)

SHOOTING THE CHUTES AT ROCK SPRINGS PARK, CHESTER, W. VA.

A curved bottom ramp caused the Chutes boats to skip across the water, a design inspired while inventor Capt. Paul Boynton, was watching boys skipping stones across a pond. The boats hopped across the 200-foot lagoon guided by a boatman standing at the aft end of the watercraft.

At the top of the Chutes ride, boatmen in sailor suits and ride operators pose with their wooden craft. On the earliest of these rides, a donkey pulled the boats to the top of the structure; however, in Rock Springs Park, each boat was carried to the top of the ramp by an electric chain lift and placed on a turntable.

The Casino, Rock Springs.

The Casino, seen here at the foot of the Chutes reflecting pool, opened on April 21, 1906, at a cost of $25,000. It replaced the original main pavilion constructed by J. E. McDonald in 1897. The first floor of this stately structure included a Japanese tea garden, six bowling alleys, a billiard hall, a shooting gallery, a barbershop, bathrooms, and park offices. The second floor could be reached by an interior staircase, and later by an exterior bridge, as seen in the picture below of the Grand Army of the Republic (GAR), a fraternal organization composed of veterans of the Union army who had served in the American Civil War.

The second floor of the Casino was devoted entirely to a 18,000-square-foot dance floor, an area large enough to permit as many as 750 couples to dance to the latest music. The neoclassical Casino was an ornately decorated open-air structure. In December 1914, it was destroyed by fire. The following season, the summer theater was used as the dance hall until another structure could be built.

Rock Springs Park, W. Va. Interior Dancing Pavilion.

The formal flowerbeds and landscaped grounds remained an important element in the overall presentation of the park during the Smith era. In 1906, park management announced that "a carload of flowers and 30,000 shrubs were being planted throughout the grounds."

Ladies Rest House, Rock Springs Lake, Chester, W. Va.

This floral postcard shows the Ladies Rest House, a necessary break room for women in corsets. The building was still being used as a restroom during the park's final year of operation and still had the original high-tank pull-chain toilets.

Four

C. C. AND GRACE MACDONALD YEARS
1926–1934

Although their years at Rock Springs Park were relatively few, Charles Clinton (C. C.) and Grace Macdonald left an indelible mark on Rock Springs and the landscape of Chester. Their efforts brought the Cyclone roller coaster, the classic 1927 Dentzel carousel, the Virginia Gardens ballroom, the Green Lantern Restaurant, and the rustic log house.

The first three seasons of the Macdonald era were quite successful, with former owner C. A. Smith commenting on July 4, 1927, that the crowd was the largest he had ever seen within the gates of the park at the noon hour. Even the perpetual thorn in the side of park owners was removed in 1929, when the Pennsylvania Railroad restored excursion rates and large group outings once again came to the park. But the Macdonalds' boon was short-lived due to the accelerated national financial crisis and the eventual stock market crash on October 24, 1929.

Even though people did, as Roy Cashdollar pointed out, "spend money for amusement when they should spend it on other things," it was only the Macdonalds' business savvy and honest dealings with contractors and suppliers that kept the park from going under during the Great Depression. Son Richard (R. Z.) Macdonald explained, "When the banks closed my father was left penniless. He owed money for the dance hall and the roller coaster and went around to creditors to try and find someone to rent the park, but there were no takers." Macdonald did not declare bankruptcy but instead promised all those who contributed materials and labor that he would repay them, or they could have the park. It took decades, but every cent was repaid. Macdonald booked showboats to take trips to the park from Pittsburgh and offered the site for camping trips where a visitor could "pitch his tent and camp in the primitive or de lux as he wishes." During the off-season, Macdonald worked at the Motor Square Gardens, a large Pittsburgh building owned by the Mellon family where car shows and marathon dances were held. Richard B. Mellon liked Macdonald's work and asked him to help modernize Idlewild Park. For four years, beginning in 1931, the Macdonalds divided their time and resources between Idlewild Park in Ligonier, Pennsylvania, and Rock Springs in West Virginia. At the end of that time, a new generation stepped in at Rocks Springs Park.

Charles (C. C.) Macdonald and his wife, Grace, found themselves enchanted with Rock Springs Park in 1926. A promotional flyer issued and signed by then-president C. C. Macdonald describes Rock Springs as "Natures Beauty Spot" and declares it "A Place Where God and Man Went Fifty-Fifty to Produce Perfection." To aid the reader, Macdonald goes on to explain that "Nature had provided everything in the way of a wondrous scenic setting, while the ingenuities of man have been devoted to the building of everything in the way of modern amusement devices and the construction of trails and walks throughout this wonderland to make these beauties more accessible to the visitor. And in the heart of this scenic wonderland, mirrored in the placid waters of the Spring Lake Lagoon, are the Rock Springs Amusements, where everything in up to date rides have been constructed for the entertainment of the public." (Left courtesy of Tish Hand.)

The Macdonalds developed a strong appreciation for rustic log structures during their years at Rock Springs Park and may have been influenced by the many log buildings found there, such as the Rustic House, pictured above. They had also spent winters at a hunting lodge in El Paso, Texas, and many of the cabin furnishings were purchased there. However, it is most likely the Macdonalds' annual hunting trips to Canada were the real reason for the attraction to log buildings. (Courtesy of Christian Comm.)

ROCK SPRINGS PARK, CHESTER, W. VA.

The Macdonalds' log cabin was erected in 1927. R. Z. Macdonald explained the origins of the house. "My dad would make hunting trips to Canada—New Brunswick. He hired Canadians to build the log house on the spot in Rock Springs Park when I was five years old." The log house rested on the hillside of the upper park facing the midway until it was moved 100 yards by crane and truck in 1974 to avoid what Roy C. Cashdollar termed "the path of progress." It remains the only structure from Rock Springs Park still in existence today and is one of the first sights people see when they cross the Ohio River into West Virginia via the Jennings Randolph Bridge.

In the 1920s, the steamer *Homer Smith* made daily excursion trips to Rock Springs Park from the foot of Smithfield Street on the Monongahela Wharf in Pittsburgh. The *Sun Telegraph* of June 6, 1928, announced that "Captain Homer Smith planned an all-day ride of 100 miles to Rock Springs Park, Chester, W.Va., on July 4."

The *Sun Telegraph* added, "Duquesne Commendery [*sic*], Knights Templar, have the boat chartered for Monday night. On Tuesday night the Craft Club of Crafton will be on board. Wednesday night the Fraternal Patriotic American Star of the West Council No. 465, will have its annual outing and on Thursday night the Carnegie Review, No. 134, Women's Benefit Association will hold its annual excursion. Merrill's Orchestra plays nightly for the dancers. Spend this afternoon on the steamer *Homer Smith*; leaves 2:30—returns 6. Night trip 8:30—back 11:30."

Two young ladies in cloche hats pose for the camera in the dance hall on board the *Homer Smith*. A raised platform at center contains various instruments, music stands, and a spotlight used by Everett Merrill's Orchestra. Signs remind passengers that there is no smoking in the dance hall, while electric fans line the walls and hang from the ceilings. A gentleman can be seen relaxing on the shaded outer deck through the open double doors at right.

Viewing benches, lifeboats, and a small boy tipping his chair are visible on the upper deck of the *Homer Smith*. In the background, the Grant Building, one of the first early-modern-style skyscrapers, is being erected above the Pittsburgh skyline. Completed in 1928, the Grant Building was Pittsburgh's tallest until it was surpassed by the Gulf Building in 1932. The new building was named for James Grant, whose advance guard in the attack on Fort Duquesne in 1758 was routed by the French. On the roof of the completed building is the world's largest neon air beacon, spelling out "Pittsburgh" in Morse code.

C. C. Macdonald fills a feed bucket in the back of his pickup truck in the Rock Springs Park zoo. Macdonald brought a strong work ethic with him when he became the manager of Rock Springs Park. According to Tish Hand, "C. C. would have worked right along with everyone else. The whole family was raised [with the ethic], 'Don't let your help do anything you wouldn't do yourself.' " It was a philosophy that would reap benefits during Macdonald's first season as operator. According to a July 1927 *East Liverpool Review* article that reported, "A crowd estimated at 20,000 people visited Rock Springs Park yesterday. Many of the visitors remained for the fireworks display last night. Dancing was held in the afternoon and evening. One hundred thousand people are expected to visit Rock Springs Park during the remainder of July, park officials said. More than a score of picnics have already been booked and others will be arranged later in the season. Fireworks will be a weekly feature, manager C. C. Macdonald has announced." (Courtesy of Tish Hand.)

This photograph clearly illustrates the transition between the Smith and the Macdonald years at Rock Springs Park. Here the Shoot-the-Chutes ride has been reduced to a pile of timbers beneath the arched bridge supports, its splash lagoon drained and a go-cart-style track under construction within its walls. To the left is the newly constructed Cyclone roller coaster, and in the background the familiar white ballroom has been improved, enlarged, and renamed "Virginia Gardens" in honor of C. C. Macdonald's 18-year-old daughter. Her younger brother, R. Z. Macdonald, remembers the dance hall as a roller skating rink. "It was a happy place for me. I considered myself to be very proficient on skates in the two-step, waltz, etc." (Courtesy of George Allison.)

During the Macdonald era, the upper park became an eclectic mix of the old and the new. The new ballroom and Cyclone roller coaster fill the background of this busy scene, while the old carousel pavilion and bridge supports stand as reminders of the park's Victorian roots. At center is a monkey cage on a small fountain island that led to the small zoo on the hill. An advertisement for the 1928 season lists these features as "Monkey Island" and "Goat Mountain." One distinguishing characteristic of the Macdonald park is the red-and-green-striped roofs of its main buildings.

Park Entrance, Chester, W. Va.

7614

It is no great coincidence that the same year Rock Springs Park saw record attendance was the year the popular Cyclone roller coaster was introduced. The "Cyclone Coaster," as one vintage brochure referred to it, was "a basic out-and-back style roller coaster designed by Harry C. Baker." Baker also designed Coney Island's Cyclone that same year. Rock Springs Park's Cyclone ran for the last time on Labor Day 1970, but Coney Island's keeps rolling along, thanks to its status as a New York City landmark.

Although the Cyclone was of a simple design, it used the unique terrain of Rock Springs Park and downtown Chester to full effect, following the hillside and dropping into a ravine behind Virginia Gardens before sending passengers flying high above Carolina Avenue and around the final bend shown here. James "Del" Cooper recalls riding the Cyclone in 1928. "All I needed was two nickels and a bottle cap to take a ride." (Courtesy of Tish Hand.)

60

It may have been this funnel-shaped collection of wooden supports that was the inspiration for the name " Cyclone" or just the feeling of being pulled into a twister as one rounded the bend high above Carolina Avenue. Either way, many have described this section of the roller coaster ride as extremely hairy. Dan Omlor of Coraopolis, Pennsylvania, said "The last car of that thing was a heart attack. It was the end of my mother's roller coaster career; she and my dad rode it after dark one Labor Day evening and she staggered off swearing she'd never ride another coaster. And she never did."

The *Beaver Daily Times* reported on May 17, 1928, that a ride on the Cyclone was the first stop for many Rock Springs Park thrill-seekers during the early Macdonald years. "On a trip through the park—first it's the Cyclone Coaster—a bell rings and the brilliantly colored cars start up the incline. Before you go down the first breath-taking dip you get a birdseye view of the park with its sparkling myriad lights and amusements." On the fifth drop of the Cyclone seen at left, brave riders raise a hand and keep the other firmly on the cross bar as the coaster cars drop into the ravine approaching Carolina Avenue and the last bend of the Cyclone. This was a point at which many have admitted to simply hanging on for dear life and hoping not to die. Below, riders pull out of the final turn and are relieved to spy the loading platform ahead. (Left courtesy of Tish Hand; below courtesy of Rich Brookes.)

AMUSEMENT CENTER SHOWING THE CYCLONE COASTER, ROCK SPRINGS PARK, CHESTER, W. VA.

The sign below the Ferris wheel beckons visitors to buy ride tickets and "See Three States." Once at the top, rocking couples could catch a stunning glimpse of West Virginia, Ohio, and Pennsylvania, as well as the beautiful Ohio River. Ticket booths, like the one in this postcard picture, were found throughout the park; also shown, from left to right, are the Aeroplane, the Whip, and the Cyclone.

ROCK SPRINGS PARK, CHESTER, W. VA.

This photograph from the Macdonald years makes an interesting contrast to the idyllic image above. Many of the same rides are visible; however this card also includes a view of an aerial joy ride known as the Octopus.

Air View—ROCK SPRINGS PARK, Chester, W. Va.

HISTORIC Rock Springs Park on the Catawba Trail. Here was the rendezvous of this tribe famed as the allies of the colonist in the Revolution. "Here they waited for the ford in the Ohio." Near the entrance to the Park, Colonel Geo. Washington and his party, including the Indians, Half King, Pheasant and White Feather, camped on the night of October 21st., 1770.

EXCURSIONS · PICNICS · TOURISTS

Unlike other sources which claim that George Washington "may have" or "reportedly" visited the springs at Rock Springs Park, this advertisement postcard issued during the Macdonald years clearly states that George Washington did indeed camp near the entrance to the park on the night of October 21, 1770. The aerial view shows the delineation between the lower park on the left and the upper park on the right. Still visible in the lower park are the white arches of the entrance gate, lily pond, bathhouse, pool, and lake. In the upper park is the Cyclone roller coaster bending in a reverse L shape past Virginia Gardens Dance Hall, the octagonal carousel pavilion, the circular monkey cage, and the Ladies Rest House. It was during this time that C. C. Macdonald built a restaurant called the Green Lantern near the trolley loop entrance—the same spot where Washington reputedly camped.

ROCK SPRINGS PARK
5 CENTS
STUDENT
RIDE TICKET
GOOD FOR 5c VALUE
ON ALL RIDES
NOT GOOD FOR
REFRESHMENTS OR GAMES
A01654 3

Admission to the park was always free. Tickets like the one shown above could be purchased for rides only. Students would find park tickets in their final report card envelopes and many, like Roy C. Cashdollar, fondly recall "the school picnics, the little zoo at the end of lovers' lane, the huge swimming pool next to the lake and the island, the restaurant in the loop at the lower entrance, roller skating in the dance hall, the penny arcade, and of course the free ice cream and goodies from Golden Star Dairy and Heinz Company Picnic Days."

During the Macdonald years, the second bathhouse sign read "Crystal Pool." The pool continued to be a great place to cool off during hot weather and included a large fountain in the center. In the background above, cars can be seen passing by on the transcontinental Route 30, the Lincoln Highway. The Lincoln Highway was rerouted on a northwesterly path from Pittsburgh through Imperial to Clinton, Pennsylvania. It eventually entered West Virginia at the lake end of Rock Springs Park, following Taylor Road past C. A. Smith's house. Smith was said to have used his political clout to lobby for this West Virginia alignment, with West Virginia the last state to be added to the Lincoln Highway in 1927.

A swarm of young schoolchildren are led by a park security officer past the Virginia Gardens Dance Hall, painted green. Several boys carry balsa-wood airplanes, which may have been a free park incentive. Whatever draws the young people forward must have been exciting, as they seem to be wholeheartedly ignoring the ice cream stand in the distance. The electric lampposts were added during the Macdonald years and allowed for later operating hours.

During the 1920s, young people frequented Virginia Gardens for its dance hall and roller skating rink. Friday night dances often featured contests in which winning couples would be brought to the stage for recognition.

In 1931, just five years after being named lessee, Macdonald became interested in Idlewild Park in Ligonier, Pennsylvania. The Macdonalds and their two sons, Richard (R. Z.) and Jack, pulled up stakes and moved to Ligonier. In the photograph below, Grace Macdonald, who spent the next four years dividing her time between the sister parks, stands proudly in front of an early Idlewild station wagon. These "woodies" were often used by railway stations for hauling luggage and petty shipments, hence the name station wagon. (Courtesy of Tish Hand.)

Five

ROBERT AND VIRGINIA HAND YEARS
1935–1970

While the Hand years have been described as "modest" ones, they were profitable. In fact, the *Billboard* reported on July 20, 1946, that Rock Springs Park "played host to more than 30,000 customers on July 4," adding that the park "remains the only funspot of several operated two decades ago between Pittsburgh and Wheeling in the Upper Ohio Valley." That same year the Hands purchased all the buildings in the park. The family's commitment to Rock Springs and the community at large kept the park going longer than most other trolley parks of the period. Twin sisters Ina and Nina France, longtime Chester residents, praise the Hands' generosity toward the community, recalling that Robert L. Hand gave their father park land on which to rebuild when their own family home collapsed during a bad storm in the 1930s. "He even let Daddy build a motel there to help him get back on his feet. Can you imagine how our Daddy must have felt when Mr. Hand told him that?" The house still stands today at the eastern end of Indiana Avenue.

The Hands' sons, Richard K. and Robert M., grew up in Rock Springs Park, and while living in a log cabin on the grounds of an amusement park made them the envy of the neighborhood, it wasn't all fun and games. The boys worked in the park from age eight through high school. Robert graduated from Chester High School in 1956, while his younger brother Richard attended Greenbrier Military Academy, where he graduated as class valedictorian in 1961.

By the late 1960s, the politically connected Robert L. Hand was aware that a new bridge and highway project would likely go right through the middle of his park. After 35 years of devoted effort, it was time to say goodbye. With their boys grown, the Hands looked forward to a long retirement together in Florida. Unfortunately Robert Hand passed away in October 1970 due to complications from a heart attack, and Virginia was left to handle all the affairs with help of her eldest son, Robert M. In less than four years, the park rides and buildings would be auctioned off to the highest bidder, and the park once described as "Nature's Beauty Spot" would be erased like a chalkboard.

This 1938 photograph of Virginia and Robert L. Hand was taken in the area between the park office and Virginia Gardens. The Hands became managers of Rock Springs Park in 1935, eventually purchasing the rides in 1946 and gaining full ownership in 1950. Behind the young couple is the final turn of the Cyclone. Below, the familiar stone fountain bubbles on the main lawn in front of the dance hall named in honor of Virginia Macdonald-Hand. (Left courtesy of Tish Hand; below, courtesy of Rich Brookes.)

The 12-car Whip provided thrills at 10¢ a ride. The Whip was invented by William F. Mangels, who also built the frame for the Dentzel carousel in Rock Springs Park. (Courtesy of Tish Hand.)

The Aeroplane swings out over the Whip and the ticket booth in this photograph taken around 1940. This ride, like a number of others, was left from the Macdonald years. The Hands were able to maintain these classic rides for 35 years, and it was for this reason that amusement park enthusiasts came to Rock Springs Park in the late 1960s. Many wanted one last chance to ride all their childhood favorites. (Courtesy of Tish Hand.)

One of the features the Hands added to the upper park was the band shell, seen here under construction in 1940. Music and live performance was always part of Rock Springs Park. In the early years, big band orchestras performed, including Glenn Miller, Tommy Dorsey, Jimmy Dorsey, Gene Krupa, and Harry James, while in later years, entertainers like Aretha Franklin and Motown's Junior Walker and the All Stars headlined along with Porky Chedwick of WAMO. (Courtesy of Tish Hand.)

Raising a family in Rock Springs Park meant park pets, including "guard geese" named Jim, Jam, Jelly, and Bread, and Great Danes like the one pictured here with Robert M. (left) and Richard K. Hand. In later years, the Hands had two Dobermans, and anyone who considered sneaking into the park at that time had to contend with the thought that they were guarding the property. Bill Gray, who worked in the park from 1953 to 1954, tells the story of a worker who closed the park and instead of going home went to the phone booth next to Virginia Gardens to make a call. Thinking his employee had gone, Bob Hand turned off the lights and released the dogs, which in turn trapped the unfortunate man in the phone booth all night. (Courtesy of Tish Hand.)

Pictured is the 1957 Golden Jubilee of Chester Dance Court. From left to right are (seated) Janet Bryant, Margaret Cline, Roxanne Erlitz, Marlene Gibbs, Joyce Mosser, Shirley McCauley, Vicki McHenry, Linda McClung, Sue Ridenger, and Suzanne Simcox; (standing) Richard Parsons, Ronald Gibbs, Frank Ravelle, David Hornick, two unidentified, Kenneth Gessford, Kenneth McClung, William Householder, and Elmer Merchant. In 1957, Bobby Vinton, a popular crooner and native of Canonsburg, Pennsylvania, provided the music for weekly dances at Rock Springs Park. It was this era he recalled in a Mountaineer Casino Racetrack and Resort press release in May 2004: "The Rock Springs Park dances were a very romantic time with the music . . . almost like something in the movies. There was the carousel, the guys in white shoes, and girls that were all dressed up with their crinoline skirts." (Courtesy of the Memory Lane Collection.)

The Cyclone loading platform is shown here with a fresh coat of paint. A ticket booth is beyond the mature trees of the upper park, and to the right is the carousel pavilion. (Courtesy of Christian Comm.)

Both Richard (R. Z.) Macdonald (pictured here with nephew Richard K. Hand) and brother-in-law Robert L. Hand served in the armed forces during World War II. Macdonald, who had a lifelong interest in aviation, was 20 years old when he joined the U.S. Air Force, while Hand was drafted and spent several months in the U.S. Army until it was discovered that he was too old for the draft. Rock Springs Park remained closed during the war, and until her husband returned, Virginia Hand spent several months in Ligonier with her parents. By the winter of 1946, the family was back in the log cabin and continued operating Virginia Gardens, with plans to reopen the entire park the following summer. (Courtesy of Tish Hand.)

During the war years, the carousel pavilion was boarded up and the portable rides stored inside. The lower park did not recover from the lack of use during the war: the swimming pool never reopened due to the shortage of materials needed for repairs after the war, and although boating continued for a time, the lake was drained significantly, effectively eliminating the small island.

In this photograph, Virginia Hand waits expectantly at the window of the Rustic House, perhaps for her husband's return from the war effort. The Macdonalds gave the cabin to their daughter and Robert L. Hand in 1935, and it served as the family's home for the next 35 years. (Courtesy of Tish Hand.)

Not to be outdone, a young Robert L. Hand displays his own station wagon with the name "Rock Springs" on the door. In the background is the building known as the office. During the summer months, a small room in this building served as a "medicine room" and is remembered by many for a moose-leg table where children sat to have their skinned elbows and knees patched up. C. C. Macdonald, an avid hunter who made frequent trips to Canada, shot the moose whose feet were used in the table. The table is now among several pieces from the park in Tish Hand's collection. In 1968, Tish Hand and her husband, Richard K., lived in the small apartment on the second floor. Hand recalled, "I lived above the office when Robert C. Hand (my first son) was two. The roller coaster's north curve was only 10 feet from my window and roared by on the weekends." (Courtesy of Tish Hand.)

Young Richard K. Hand must have been considered one of the luckiest kids in the world by his peers. Not only did he get to grow up in an amusement park, but he also got to ride this cool 1940s-era Colson chain-driven tricycle. This winter photograph shows the upper entrance of Rock Springs Park beneath the third drop of the Cyclone. Virginia Gardens is visible through the gate. The bike could have been a Christmas or a birthday present, as Hand was born on New Year's Day 1943. (Courtesy of Tish Hand.)

Below, an interior view of the same entrance can be seen. In this earlier photograph, a white archway with flashing lights greeted visitors to the park who would then walk under carloads of screaming riders. The freshly painted white waiting platform awaits the red letters spelling out Cyclone, which were detailed above the stairway.

The cement staircase and walls in both of these photographs are remnants of the early-20th-century Shoot-the-Chutes, while the Aerial Joy Ride was added during the Hand years. The Aerial Joy Ride was a popular favorite, because riders could generate their own thrills while piloting and maneuvering their spinning airplane.

Bob Hand, seen here along the midway, always worked in the park on the weekends. Virginia was usually in the office and took care of the medicine room. Chester resident Dick McGurren also worked at the park. With only one lung due to a war injury, employment for McGurren at one of the local potteries or steel mills was impossible, but he loved his job in the outdoors at Rock Springs. To many of the kids that came to park, it seemed that McGurren was the owner, not just a trusted employee and manager. Richard K. Hand referred to him as "Uncle Dick" and commented often that he almost raised him, and R. Z. Macdonald (the real "Uncle Dick") remembers McGurren as a "high-class fellow." (Courtesy of Tish Hand.)

The Octopus would raise and spin passengers toward the treetops, as depicted in this undated photograph. (Courtesy of Tish Hand.)

In later years, the Hands wintered in Florida, but when the boys were younger, the family spent Christmases warmed by the stone fireplace in the living room of the log cabin. The fireplace went two stories up to the peak of the beamed ceiling, with a small window to each side. A cast-iron chandelier hung from the ceiling, and in his younger days, Richard K. would jump from the balcony and swing on the chandelier like a motion picture swashbuckler. The chandelier was six feet across and made for candles, with little cups that could be dropped down to put the candles out at night. Pictured here from left to right are Robert M., Richard K., Virginia, and Robert L. (Courtesy of Tish Hand.)

Every year, a live blue spruce was decorated for the holidays in the living room and then planted outside the log house along the front wall. Tish Hand noted that the evergreens seem to "stand like sentinels to many Christmases gone by." (Courtesy of Rich Brookes.)

Robert M. Hand was five years older than his brother. Here he poses in front of a series of green park benches that were eventually sold in public auction. One of these benches, donated by Lou and Helen Eskra, is now on display in the Chester Municipal Building less than 100 yards from where this photograph was taken. (Courtesy of Tish Hand.)

Upon the release of the large wooden brake, riders onboard the Cyclone would have gently descended in their red car from the loading platform heading toward this slight bend in the tracks.

Here the cars pass under the second drop before locking into place at the foot of the chain lift hill.

This view taken from the Chester High School parking lot and the close-up view below show the long, slow ascent of the Cyclone's chain lift hill at the end of a tree-lined Louisiana Avenue. Many residents along this street remember vividly the summertime sights, sounds, and smells of living next to an amusement park. Mike West grew up there and recalled, "We lived only 100 yards from the Cyclone, and at night in the summer with the windows open, I would fall asleep listening to the rattle of the chain drive and the scream of the patrons as they went down the first hill."

Beyond the line of green park benches and the remains of the concrete bridge supports, one can see the first turn of the Cyclone. Riders who were able to keep their eyes open could catch a glimpse of the beautiful upper park, downtown Chester, the Ohio River, and the hills of East Liverpool before taking the sudden plunge.

Riders flying over the second hill of the Cyclone speed past the Turnpike Junior. Chester High School is visible in the background on the right.

Guests eager for their turn on the Cyclone gather at the waiting station in the background. Screams of riders and the thunder-like rumble of cars speeding past only added to the excitement. In the foreground, parents watch as their child takes a ride on the Kiddie Whip.

In this photograph from the 1960s, an automobile can be seen passing by the Cyclone roller coaster on Carolina Avenue. To the left is the yellow brick trolley entrance, and through the crosshatched supports to the final turn of the Cyclone, the Virginia Gardens Dance Hall can be seen.

Cyclone cars streak past the northern side of Virginia Gardens. Note that two riders chose to sit in the front and two in the back of the otherwise empty car. Coaster enthusiasts cite these as the best seats to experience thrills and "airtime."

In this photograph, two brave passengers have their hands in the air, increasing the adrenaline rush on this classic wooden coaster.

Here a park employee sits almost casually in the front seat. From this point the ride makes a left beside Virginia Gardens and returns riders gently to the waiting station.

Bob Hand readies snow cones for guests looking for a cool and tasty treat in 1968. Snow cones were first served from an ice machine in the park in 1920. (Courtesy of Tish Hand.)

The lunch stand, in the foreground, served such favorites as hot dogs and hamburgers. Here a few park patrons stop for a snack, while others head toward the carousel pavilion in the background.

The 153 Wurlitzer Band Organ can be seen behind three rows of rare Daniel Muller–designed horses in this photograph from the Hand years. Muller studied sculpture at the Pennsylvania Academy of Fine Arts, where he developed an interest in the U.S. cavalry horses of the Civil War. Military mounts like the ones pictured above became his trademark. Several of these horses were showcased in Tobin Fraley's book *The Carousel Animal* in 1987.

The carousel featured 48 horses, including "standers," like the one pictured above. These horses stood stationary, and although not as thrilling to ride as the jumpers, they gave riders on the outer rim a chance to grab for the brass ring, which could be used for a free ride or kept as a good luck charm.

In June 1974, the Smithsonian Institute inspected the 1927 Dentzel carousel for purchase. According to the *Panhandle Press*, the institute hoped to place it near the National Mall in Washington, D.C., "as a living monument to the past." When Robert W. Mason of the Smithsonian decided against its purchase due to its lack of menagerie animals and relatively plain rounding board, dealer Jim Wells of Fairfax, Virginia, who had accompanied Mason, bought it. The carousel then changed hands several times and eventually became part of the Freels Foundation's American Carousel Museum in San Francisco, a nonprofit organization for the preservation of carousels. On June 13, 1998, it was sold at auction along with most of the museum's rare Daniel Muller horses. On its Web site, Brass Ring Entertainment of Sun Valley, California, the present owner of the Dentzel, is offering the carousel with a combination of original and reproduction horses at an estimated cost of $1.5 million. The photograph below shows Dick McGurren on the Dentzel carousel at the time of the Smithsonian inspection. (Below courtesy of Mary Jane Dickey.)

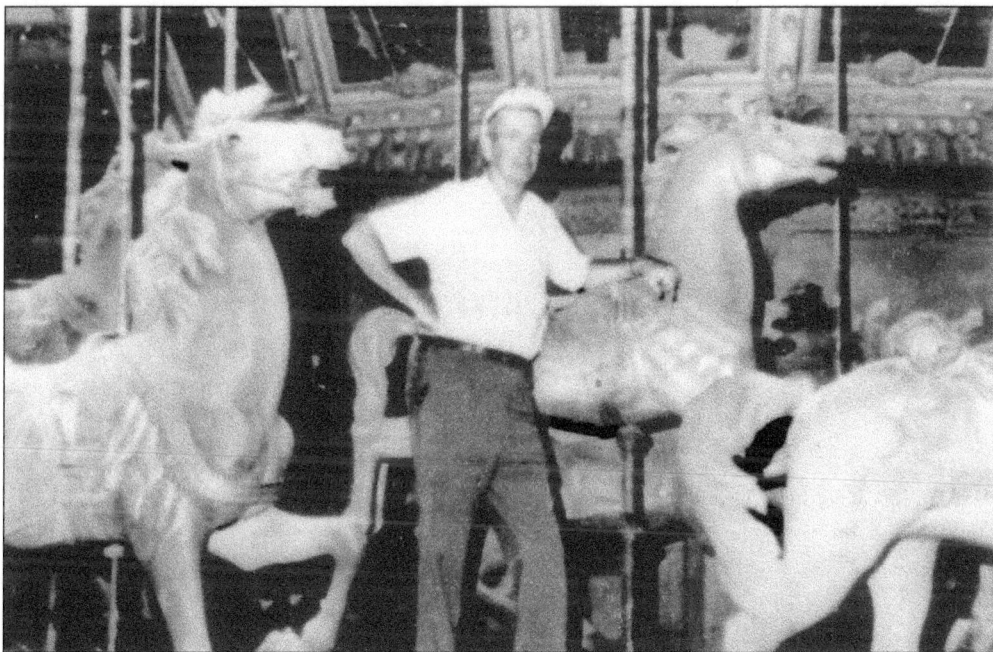

Walter Thompson can be seen at right operating the popular Aeroplane. The aerial ride simulated the experience of a vintage open-cockpit airplane. The underside of the plane above reveals gaps in the wooden floorboards, which would have allowed riders a limited view of the spinning ground. In the photograph below, airplanes soar beyond the elevated loading platform suspended by cables, while a dizzying circus march with its bass-heavy "Oom Paa Paa" plays from the carousel band organ in the distance. (Below courtesy of Rich Brookes.)

Richard Hand works the cash register at the ball toss along the midway in the summer of 1968. The sign reads "Over 12 Wins Choice." (Courtesy of Tish Hand.)

Across the midway from the ball toss, Karen Sayre helps a young patron and his parents identify the prize-winning number on a plastic duck. The Duck Pond game was one of the simplest crowd-pleasers at the park, because, as this photograph suggests, even the youngest child could play. In the distance are the carport and the Dodgem cars. (Courtesy of Rich Brookes.)

Miniature cars were a popular fixture at the park during the Hand years. Above, a small boy turns into the curve on the Kiddie Cars, while below, the turnpike track winds through the mall area. The vintage 1950s automobiles were quite popular with the younger park guests even into the late 1960s and early 1970s. In the background below, from left to right, are the Dodgem car pavilion, the band shell, and the buckets (or Spinneroo ride) on a raised platform. (Above courtesy of Rich Brookes.)

Nickel pinball was one of the many games enjoyed in the arcade, shown here looking quite weathered in 1970. There were also machines that created good luck coins for 10¢. One side of the coin had a lucky horseshoe and on the other side an American flag. A hand lever was pulled down to imprint a customer's name on the coin. To the right of the arcade in this photograph is a game stand where customers threw darts at balloons.

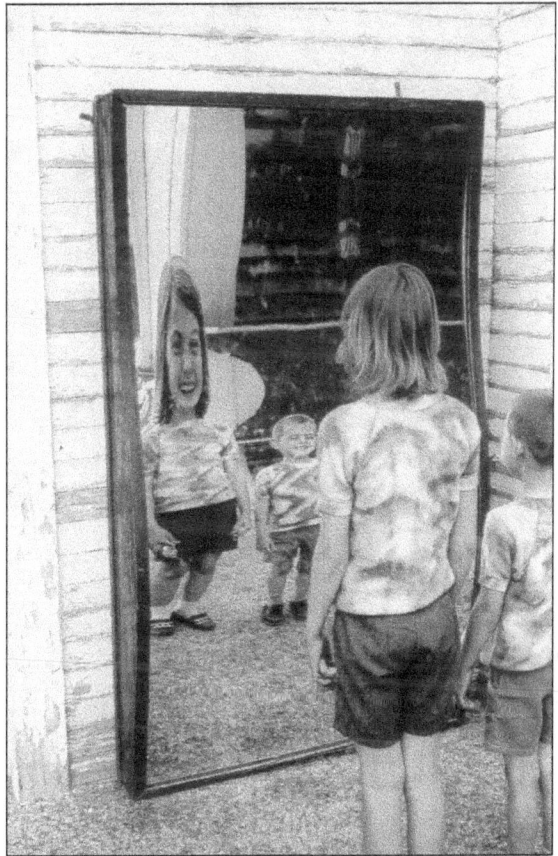

Originally the arcade housed the Rumpus, a walk-through fun house featuring a two-story slide, a spinning disk, and an array of distorting mirrors, which were removed after someone ran into one of them and was injured. Two mirrors remained on either side of the entrance to the arcade, however. Crystal Smith and her younger brother, Kippy, shown here in 1970, are amused by their reflections. (Courtesy of Rich Brookes.)

Although George Washington Gale Ferris, the inventor of the Ferris wheel, founded his company in Pittsburgh, just 40 miles southeast of Chester, Rock Springs Park's Ferris wheel was manufactured by the Eli Bridge Company of Jacksonville, Illinois. The first "Big Eli" debuted in 1900, and by 1906, the model was being mass-produced.

Billy Thorn operates the 12-seat Rock Springs Park Ferris wheel. During this time, the Ferris wheel was situated between the office and the garage.

Mary Bernardi and sons Anthony (left) and Leonard take an ice cream break near the Kiddie Whip in 1969. The park was just a short distance from the Bernardi home and business, Bernardi's Italian Restaurant, which was located on corner of Carolina Avenue and Sixth Street. (Courtesy of Rich Brookes.)

Taking a rare break from their duties as ride operators are senior park workers Ben Grimes (left), "Uncle Pete" Theiss (center), and Dick McGurren, seated on one of the benches surrounding the Kiddie Whip. In the background are the Kiddie Airplanes and the Aeroplane tower. (Courtesy of Rich Brookes.)

The Pretzel Ride, pictured above, is listed among 15 other rides on a daily receipt log used during the Hand years. The Pretzel Ride was a single-track spook house ride located on the southern end of the midway. The ride, manufactured by the Pretzel Company of Bridgeton, New Jersey, featured a large pretzel design on the side of each car and guaranteed to "Send 'Em Out Laughing."

On the midway looking toward the rustic log house, an unidentified little girl is amused by a park employee at the Duck Pond. Behind are the carport and the Dodgem cars.

This brick drive near the log cabin led to the lake and lower picnic park. Richard K. Hand had a bad spill on this path while riding his bicycle, as it was uneven at the bottom. According to Ira Sayre, most of the yellow bricks used throughout Rock Springs Park were seconds—factory bricks too good to throw out but not good enough to be sold at retail prices.

A close inspection of the "Rock Springs Park" sign on the Cyclone reveals that each letter is lined with lights. The sign glowed brightly on the evenings Rock Springs Park was open and could be seen by passing cars, boats, and the townspeople of East Liverpool on the opposite shore.

Two sets of tracks are clearly visible in the trolley loop turnaround at the end of Marks Run. It is this entrance that children from the "upper end" of Chester recall using, including Scott Beck and his friends. "We would come up through the streetcar entrance across from Chaney's gas station, past the springs, and make our way up the steps to where they were making cotton candy. I would always stop, fascinated by the process, and will always remember the smell."

By 1970, the beautiful arched gate, flower gardens, and Green Lantern Restaurant were gone from the trolley loop. However, visitors in these later years were still delighted by the fact that a yellow brick road led them into the park.

This unique curving picnic pavilion located in the lower park was still in use during the park's last season. It was one of two picnic structures that remained. Many referred to this section of Rock Springs Park as the "lower picnic area."

A view of the diminished lake in 1970 reveals a small cluster of trees in the background where Bower Island once stood.

By 1970, little evidence remained of the crystal pool and bathhouse next to the lake other than this faint outline of the foundation and a small section of wall below the tree-lined Route 30.

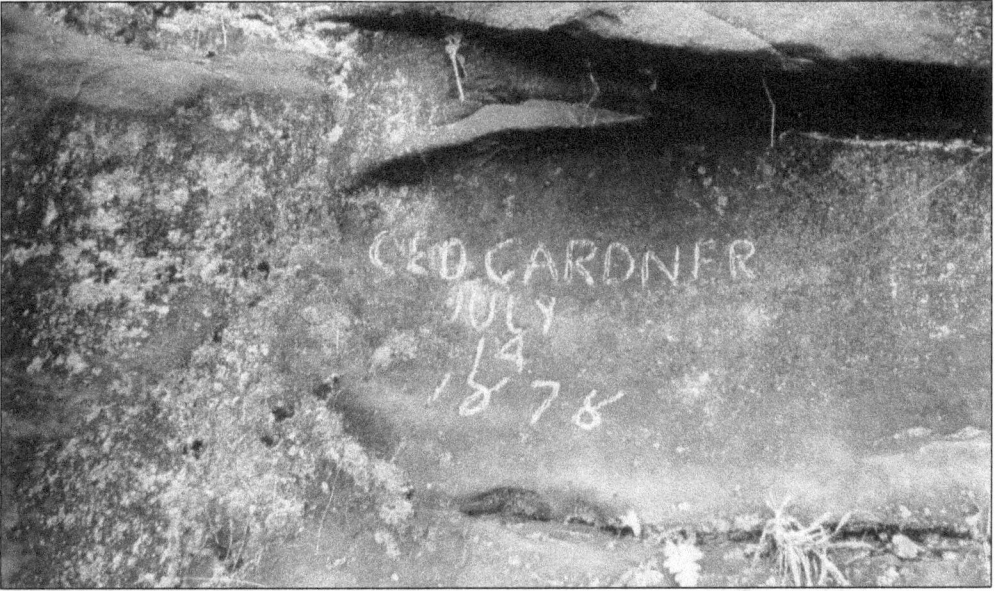

This rock was photographed in 1970 by park photographer Clarence O. Durbin. The etching was made by George Gardner, a member of one of the original nine farming families in Chester, on July 14, 1878. Although it is not visible in most early postcard pictures or photographs, the exposed rock face of Rock Springs was covered with hundreds of historic carvings like this one. Born on July 31, 1860, Gardner was just shy of 18 years old when he made his mark on the world. He died in 1922 and is now laid to rest in Riverview Cemetery in East Liverpool near a marble obelisk honoring the Gardner family. (Courtesy of Rich Brookes.)

The famous spring still gushes out of the solid rock wall in this photograph. At center are the professional stairs and in the left foreground the "On the Rocks" boulder seen in early-20th-century postcards. Here in 1970, children enjoy a drink from the springs, which continued to spill 1,000 gallons a day from deep within the mountain.

Having spent their married life as managers and owners of Rock Springs Park, Bob and Virginia Hand looked forward to a comfortable retirement in Florida. Unfortunately Robert L. Hand passed away in October 1970, and Rock Springs Park never reopened. Above, the couple, known to their grandchildren as "Bampa" and "Bammie," poses for a snapshot along the midway. Below, the structure named for Virginia Macdonald-Hand 43 years earlier awaits its future upon the park's closing. (Both courtesy of Rich Brookes.)

Six

A LONG FAREWELL
1971–1974

Rock Springs Park sat idle for four years following the death of owner Robert L. Hand, and although many of the portable rides had been sold and removed, the bare bones of the Aeroplane tower remained, with its warped and sagging round roof, and row upon row of kiddie rides rusted in the overgrown grass of the upper park mall. The Cyclone and all of the buildings, including the spook house and the boarded-up octagonal carousel building with its hand-carved horses and 153 Wurlitzer Band Organ still locked inside, remained frozen in time, ghostly reminders of the park's magical past.

In the summer of 1974, the park would be reawakened for one last fling for "old times' sake." Hundreds of people returned in June for a farewell dance at Virginia Gardens. The *Panhandle Press* reported on June 26, 1974, "Sunday night was the 'Last Dance' at Virginia Gardens. Everyone in the surrounding area has such loving memories from years gone by, ones that will never be forgotten and after last Sunday night; more than 1,000 people added that evening to the loving memories." The proceeds from the event went to the Northern Hancock County Community Library, now the Lynn Murray Memorial Library, in Chester.

By the end of July, the twenty-one remaining structures were sold in auction for $5,200. William W. Harper, a well-known business man in Chester, bought the Virginia Gardens dance hall for $550 and William Johnson of East Liverpool bought the mile-long Cyclone for one dollar. According to the Youngstown Vindicator, Johnson planned to use the wood from the coaster to build a new structure at an auto wrecking business he and his father operated near Calcutta, OH. The deconstruction of the park was completed quickly and "within 45 days," wrote Susan Weaver, "the park was stripped of all its buildings and the bulldozers, backhoes, and earth-movers were brought in."

The weathered skeleton frame of the Cyclone roller coaster reminded people of a simpler time. This picture shows the loading platform and approach to the second hill in the early 1970s. Beyond it stands the old Chester High School.

The chain lift hill can be seen in the background of this photograph from 1973. The Cyclone ran parallel to the junior high playground, and many a stray kickball had to be extracted from its web of wooden supports.

After 47 years, the first bend and drop of the Cyclone still stands above the overgrowth of grass, weeds, shrubs, and vines. The arched bridge supports can be seen in the foreground, and in the background is a small building used as a paint shop.

The once welcoming and well-lit white arched entrance of the upper park is gone in the photograph above. In its place are "Beware of Dog" and "No Trespassing" signs. Cars belonging to planners of the Last Dance at Virginia Gardens are parked near the office.

The chain lift hill and the first drop of the Cyclone look as formidable in 1974 before the Last Dance at Virginia Gardens as they did when the park was open. Like the wooden red cars of old, the fate of Rocks Springs Park was locked in place and moving forward toward its inevitable fate. (Above courtesy of Rich Brookes; below courtesy of Dr. Mike West.)

Even in its boarded-up condition, the carousel pavilion, seen here in 1974, caught the attention of curious young schoolchildren on the nearby playground. Slightly older teenagers did sneak into the park for one last look and to nab popcorn boxes or light bulbs from the carousel as final souvenirs. It is a testament to the respect the community felt for the park, however, that after four years sitting vacant, not one of the windows in the carousel pavilion was broken. Below, Scott Paulson (left) plays at not having enough money to ride while John Sayres pantomimes buying his ride tickets. Paulson later became a Pittsburgh radio personality and morning staple on WDVE's Morning Show. (Both courtesy of Dr. Mike West.)

This aerial photograph shows Rock Springs Park after it closed in 1970. The upper entrance to the park was located at the end of Indiana Avenue just past the old Chester High School (the L-shaped building at bottom), permitting easy access to the proms held at Virginia Gardens. (Courtesy of the Memory Lane Collection.)

Clarence O. Durbin captured this view of Virginia Gardens and the green rolling hills of Chester by scaling the Cyclone tracks with his camera on Memorial Day, May 31, 1971. (Courtesy of Rich Brookes.)

This photograph from the Durbin series dramatically illustrates the height and vistas experienced by Cyclone riders on the notorious final turn above Carolina Avenue. (Courtesy of Rich Brookes.)

Carolina Avenue intersects with Route 30 and the old trolley loop across from Chaney's service station in this panorama taken at the highest point of the Cyclone turnaround. (Courtesy of Rich Brookes.)

In the background of this photograph from 1974, cars fill the parking lot of Virginia Gardens at the same time the planning committee for the Last Dance is told that the evening would have to be cancelled due to a lack of electricity. At the last minute, committee members located a generator from a local army base that was used to provide power to the ballroom. To close the evening, a 14-piece orchestra played "Auld Lang Syne" at 1:10 a.m., making it officially the last dance at Virginia Gardens. Guests did not want to leave, and many kept their tickets as mementos of their last visit to Rock Springs Park.

This circular wooden fence once enclosed the Kiddie Boats. In the background from left to right are the carousel pavilion, duck pond, ticket booth, carport, and Dodgem cars.

The buildings at left in this photograph of the midway are the lunch stand and carousel pavilion. The first building on the right featured a balloon dart game; beyond is the arcade and ball toss. (Courtesy of Dr. Mike West.)

In this opposite view, the garage is the first building at left. It housed the tractor and other lawn maintenance equipment but also "heaps and stacks of old penny arcade machines and pennylodeons," according to Tish Hand, some of which featured scantily clad ladies dancing about when a handle was turned. Next is the cotton candy and popcorn stand. (Courtesy of Dr. Mike West.)

Workers contemplate an attempt to relocate the band shell to the Chester City Park. Unfortunately the old bandstand barely survived transport and fell apart soon after. The city then built a cinder block amphitheater in its place, which now has also been removed. (Courtesy of Dr. Mike West.)

This view of the Cyclone in 1974 illustrates why it was considered an out-and-back style coaster. Here the track in the foreground would send riders out and over the hill approaching the ravine behind Virginia Gardens, and next to it the return track guided them back to the loading platform. (Courtesy of Rich Brookes.)

The arcade, in need of a good paint job during the final years of Rock Springs Park, looks spooky in this photograph taken in 1974. Many amusement parks today extend their season by offering Halloween-related activities during the fall. Based on these photographs, Rock Springs Park would have made for a terrific fright night. (Courtesy of Dr. Mike West.)

A green goblin sneers menacingly from the front of the spook house. This mural could be seen from the playground and perhaps, just as much as the Cyclone and the merry-go-round, tempted children to wander over the fence for a closer look. (Courtesy of Dr. Mike West.)

Here unchecked weeds and grasses are slowly overrunning the set of professionally poured concrete steps from the Hand era.

With its troughs and extension pipes gone, the area near the spring returned to the look it may have had in the days of George Washington and his surveying party. For many local residents, the loss of the spring and its wood grove was more devastating than that of the amusement park itself.

The office at right and the Virginia Gardens dance hall below are painted with the numbers 3 and 4 respectively. The numbers indicate the order of demolition of the remaining structures in Rock Springs Park. Even as late as June 26, 1974, there were hopes of saving Virginia Gardens with the *Panhandle Press* reporting, "Sunday night was the 'Last Dance' at Virginia Gardens, unless we are fortunate to have a local buyer of the building for community use." Nonetheless, the dance hall was bought for its lumber, especially the large beams underneath. Two features of the old ballroom were saved—the arched sign above the door and a large mirror ball.

Building No. 4, once the Ohio Valley's most beautiful ballroom, is just hours away from becoming a memory in this photograph. Mary Jane Dickey, daughter of park manager Dick McGurren, worked in the park for 35¢ an hour in her youth. "As soon as one of us could count change, Daddy had us working." Dickey flew home to Chester from Texas to attend the Last Dance, which was bittersweet for her, as she recalled the magic of the evening but also the sadness at seeing guests tearing the latticework from the walls at the end of the night. "Folks just wanted a piece of it to take with them. No one wanted to leave. After the dance we walked down the midway one last time for old time's sake."

The band shell also appears to be numbered for demolition, but a close inspection of the image reveals it to have an unpainted mark. It sold for $1, as did many of the buildings in the park in an auction held on Saturday, June 22, 1974, the day before the Last Dance. The auction also featured rides and equipment, including the Eli No. 5 Ferris wheel, the Spinnaroo with 8 tubs, 16 bumper cars, keno board, and blower, a candy apple stove, and 150 dance hall chairs, among others.

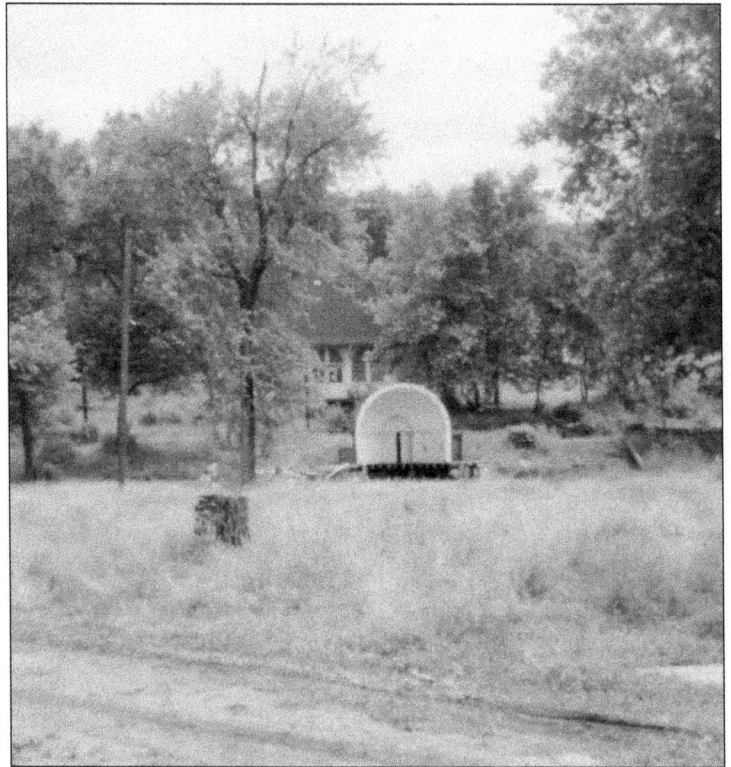

It is not an optical illusion that the rustic log cabin in the background of these two photographs appears to be in two different locations. Longtime residents of Chester Mary and Don Chaney bought the old cabin at auction. Daughter Donna Bell-Chaney reported that "Dad was able to buy some land from Virginia Hand and he engaged an outfit out of Ohio that specialized in moving historic structures. They jacked it up and transported it over to a newly excavated basement foundation. They were able to level the cabin in the process." The cabin sold for $100 but the cost to move it was $30,000. One-time owner Virginia Hand commented after the sale that the hinges on the doors were worth more than $100.

The log house and the band shell were spared, but all other structures in the park were razed. Here stacks of wood and rubble line the carport and Dodgem cars structures. Note the hand-painted sign on the back wall of the Dodgem cars that reads "No Head On Bumping." This structure sold for $1,000 in auction, more than the roller coaster, bandstand, fun house, and main office building combined. The metal flooring and required metal roofing panels are what made it so valuable.

At left, an unidentified person bends down to collect a small souvenir in an area of Rock Springs Park. Near this same spot, Richard K. Hand lost a tie tack given to him by his parents upon graduation. It was a little gold hand that held a quarter-carat diamond. He was heartbroken according to wife Tish Hand. Just before the park closed, his brother Bob was raking the gravel in front of the lunch stand and found the diamond pin. Richard's daughter, Kassy Hand, still wears it, as it was made into a necklace for her graduation.

Even before the last remains of Rock Springs Park could be removed, the main truss of the Jennings Randolph Bridge loomed in the background. At this time, the bridge stood in the waters of the Ohio River with no connection to either shore.

In 1974, the lower picnic area, shown here, was being flagged to mark the route of the new highway approach to the Jennings Randolph Bridge. Many felt that the new path of Route 30 and the approach to the bridge could have been restricted to this lower park corridor; however, planners and engineers chose to curve the highway toward the west, effectively eliminating all but a small section of the upper park.

117

Nature reclaims the trolley loop in 1974 (left), while the western shore of the spring lake lagoon (below) appears much the same as it did during the C. A. Smith years. Within a little less than one year, both areas would be rendered unrecognizable.

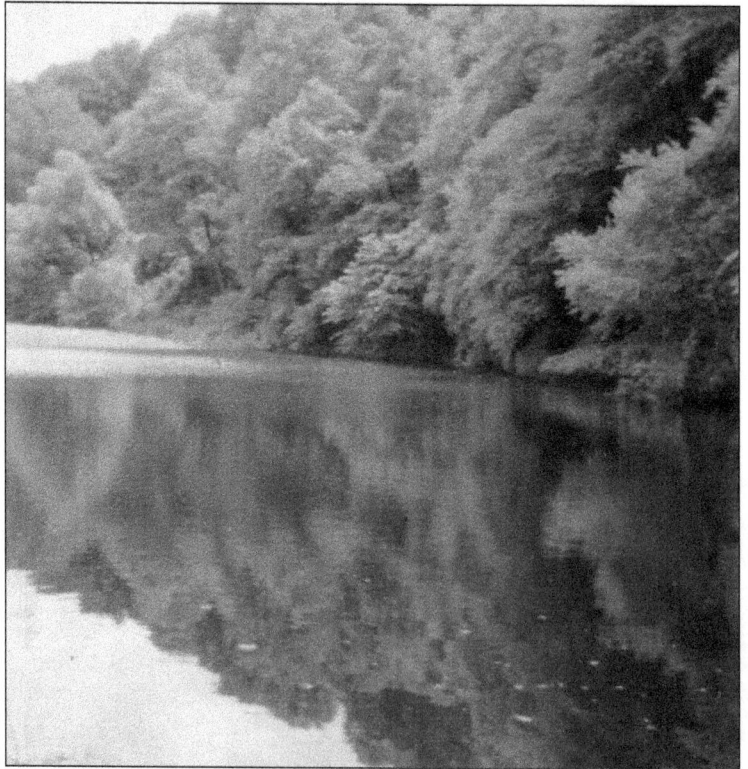

The hillside and grove of mature trees that once stood between the upper and lower sections of Rock Springs Park have been stripped away in this photograph, leaving the area of separation nearly nonexistent. The old Chester High School can be seen in the background behind what was once the midway and mall area of the main park. The huge rocks and boulders that were exposed near the original spring have been shattered and lie in a long pile of rubble in the foreground.

In the photograph at left, the lake has been drained and the mountain beyond is being cut in two. Today drivers entering Chester along Route 30 from Pennsylvania travel through this man-made pass as they approach the Jennings Randolph Bridge.

119

The photograph above shows the area of Chester where Rock Springs Park once stood. A car enters town driving through the pass created for the two-lane highway. To the driver's right is old Route 30. In the foreground, the neighborhood known locally as the "Mill Addition" includes many of the homes built for workers of the old tin mill that filled early postcard images of Rock Springs Park with black smoke. Beyond is the gazebo of the Virginia Gardens Memorial Park and Chester High School. Nestled in the trees above is the log house in its present location. (Courtesy of Margaret Comm.)

The curving double lanes of Route 30 snake through Marks Run and hide any evidence that Rock Springs Park once graced this end of Chester. The area over which the Jennings Randolph Bridge passes is the same location where steamboats like the *Senator* and the showboat *Majestic* once delivered pleasure seekers from Pittsburgh and Wheeling. Just above the bridge is the home of park owner C. A. Smith, and at left are the remains of Taylor, Smith, and Taylor (TS&T) Pottery. (Courtesy of Rob Morrow.)

120

Seven

THE MAGIC LIVES ON
1975–PRESENT

There are few reminders that Rock Springs Park ever existed. The log house, once the family home of owners Robert and Virginia Hand, is the only structure to survive the demolition, along with a few bits and pieces of the park that can be found in front yards, shop windows, and collectors' shelves. But for the incorrectly titled historical marker on Carolina Avenue which reads "Rock Spring Park," visitors to the area might never realize that Chester was once the home of the Tri-State Region's premier panhandle playground. But just ask someone in town about the park, and they will smile and tell a story about free ice cream during the Golden Star Dairy Picnic Day, grabbing for the brass ring on the merry-go-round, or staggering off the Cyclone loading platform vowing to never ride another roller coaster again and meaning it. For some, it is enough to keep the magic of the park alive with memories such as these, but for others, having a piece of the park—a postcard, a souvenir dish, a pennant, or even a cracked and faded yellow brick—brings the excitement and joy of youthful trips to the park with family and friends back to mind. This is where the magic lives, in the hearts and minds of those who knew the park and those who grew up hearing all the wonderful tales of Rock Springs Park.

The only existing structure left from Rock Springs Park is the rustic log house, pictured here in the fall of 2009. The house and the sign announcing "Almost Heaven" offer a pleasant greeting to visitors crossing the Jennings Randolph Bridge from Ohio into West Virginia. (Courtesy of Christian Comm.)

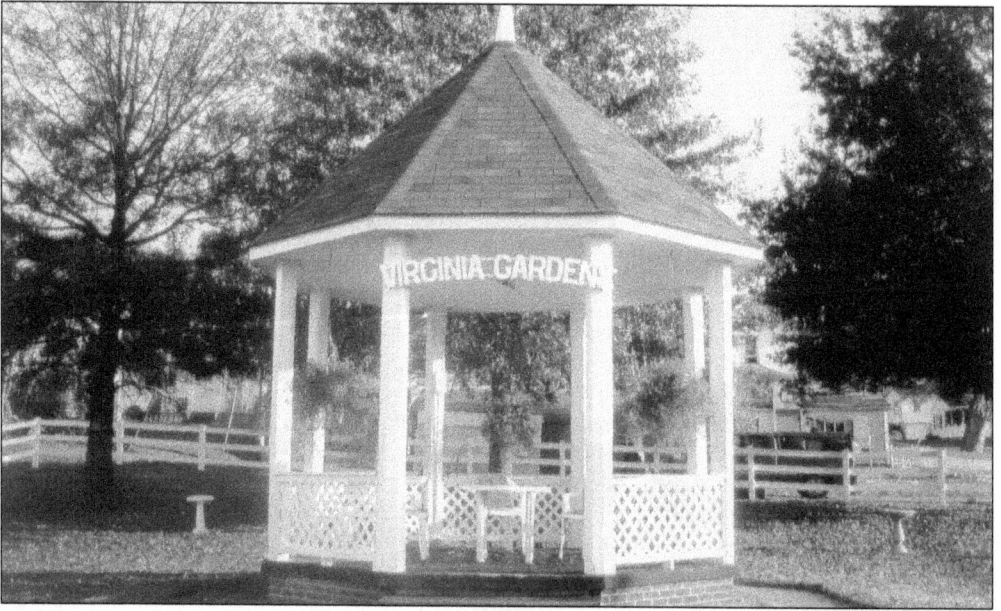

This small gazebo can be found in the Virginia Gardens Memorial Park at the corner of Carolina Avenue and Sixth Street. The park was dedicated in July 1983 as part of the first annual Rock Springs Park festival. The ceremony featured the first Miss Virginia Gardens, Lori Theiss, granddaughter of former park employee Pete Theiss. The memorial park once exhibited the original arched Virginia Gardens sign, but it was recently removed due to deterioration. A new sign, attached to the gazebo, is pictured above. The gazebo was built by Sayre W. Graham Sr., with the memorial grounds maintained by Vic Soble and the Chester Lions Club. (Courtesy of Christian Comm.)

This commemorative sign was the result of over two years of correspondence beginning September 8, 1978, between mayor Roy Cashdollar and West Virginia congressman Robert Mollohan. Cashdollar and fellow planning commission members Frank DeCapio and Rex Cowey may have been disappointed when the park was incorrectly identified as "Rock Spring" without the final "s," but residents are grateful that the site of Rock Springs Park has been permanently marked and registered with the state for future generations. (Courtesy of Christian Comm.)

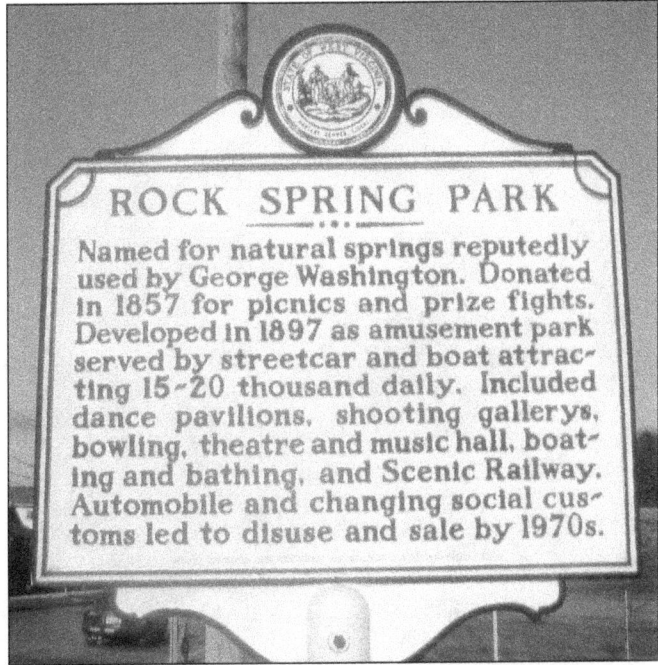

ROCK SPRING PARK

Named for natural springs reputedly used by George Washington. Donated in 1857 for picnics and prize fights. Developed in 1897 as amusement park served by streetcar and boat attracting 15~20 thousand daily. Included dance pavilions, shooting gallerys, bowling, theatre and music hall, boating and bathing, and Scenic Railway. Automobile and changing social customs led to disuse and sale by 1970s.

On the hillside east of the northbound lane of Route 30, a lone pipe still carries the fresh mineral waters of Rock Springs. At one time, the springs were thought to be medicinal. Today, however, the spring, which has never run dry, empties unceremoniously into a drainage ditch above the World's Largest Teapot. Broken yellow bricks from the trolley loop can still be found scattered throughout the site. (Courtesy of Christian Comm.)

The original mirrored ball used in Virginia Gardens still turns during dances and wedding receptions held at the American Legion Post 121 in Chester. In the photograph, Jack Sprout pulls a ladder used for hanging Christmas decorations out of the shot. Sprout explained that the legion purchased the ball at auction in 1974.

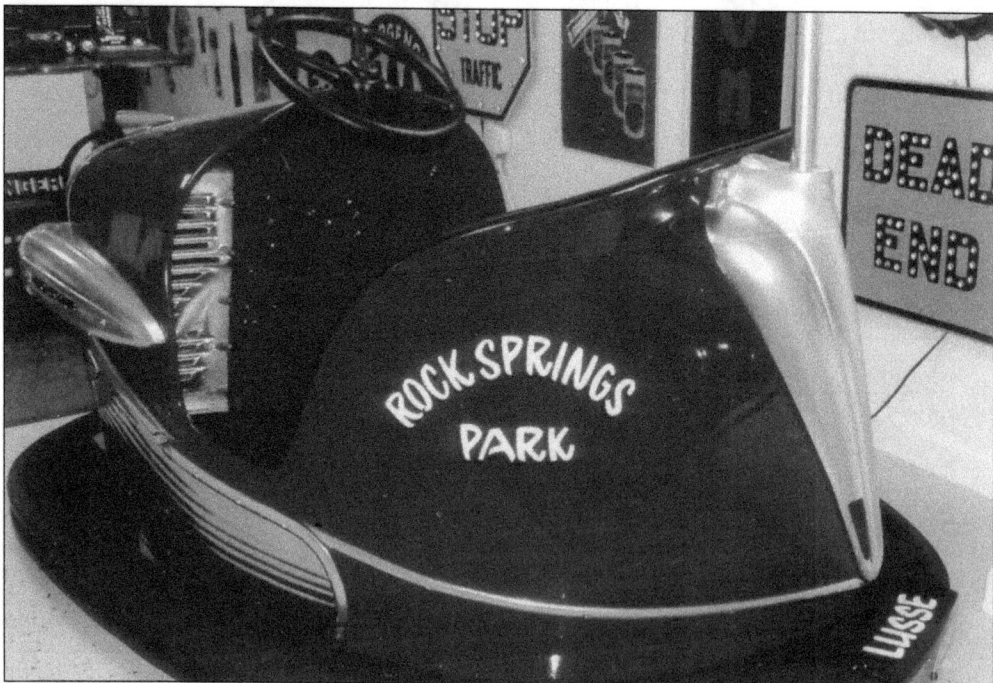

This 1941 Lusse bumper car was lovingly restored by Weirton resident David Rhoades. "I bought this car from Gary Wasmer, who bought 12 of them from Earl Cuppy about 15 years ago. I have been told Cuppy bought a lot of the rides from the park, not just the bumper cars. I went to the park when I was a kid and just wanted to have a piece of history." (Courtesy of David Rhoades.)

The ball atop the flagpole in Dean McKinney's front yard in Chester used to be one of several finials crowning the railing of the cement steps leading to Rock Springs. McKinney and his father, George, welded the ball on a section of pipe sleeve purchased at Werkheiser's Hardware. (Courtesy of Christian Comm.)

Bill and Donna Gray keep the memory of Rock Springs Park alive with their vast collection of souvenirs and memorabilia from the park. The couple enjoys sharing their collection with visitors to their Highland Colony home. Above, Gray stands next to the collection, which includes nearly 250 postcards, many fine pieces of cranberry glass and custard glass, numerous plates, several pennants, and more items too numerous to mention.

The 153 Wurlitzer Band Organ that originally played in the octagonal carousel pavilion at Rock Springs Park now plays tunes for 25¢ in the lobby of the Lou Holtz Upper Ohio Valley Hall of Fame in downtown East Liverpool. The organ was part of Dr. James Smith's vast collection of antique coin-operated machines, which he housed in a suburban barn near his Greenwich, Connecticut, home. Smith, who grew up in East Liverpool, became attracted to the band organ, the carousel, and most especially the penny and nickel arcade games of chance on his many trolley visits to Rock Springs Park during the Depression. The Wurlitzer was donated to the East Liverpool High School Alumni Association in 1994, and the rest of Smith's collection sold at Sotheby's in New York for more than $3.3 million. (Courtesy of Christian Comm.)

Number one Rock Springs Park fan Richard Bowker (right) and Charles J. Jacques Jr., author of *Kennywood—The Roller Coaster Capital of the World*, enjoy a carousel ride in Hershey Park, Pennsylvania, in 1980. Bowker visited Rock Springs Park nearly every weekend in 1970 and rode the Cyclone on its final trip on Labor Day as the lights were being turned off forever. In 2009, an 80-year-old Bowker visited the Lou Holtz Upper Ohio Valley Hall of Fame and heard his favorite 153 Wurlitzer Band Organ play again after nearly 40 years.

Volunteers Shirley Barnhart, Joyce Dotson, Anita Kukich, Mary Lawrence, Doris Whittaker, Nancy Woods, and Mary Ann Wright have devoted hundreds of hours to archiving and displaying photographs and artifacts in the Memory Lane room located in the municipal building on Indiana Avenue in Chester. The room tells the story of Chester from its start as a small farming community to its pottery industry and one-time designation as the "Show Place of the East."

People in the area fondly recall Rock Springs Park and honor its memory in many ways. Lance and Deanne Hooper, in a moment of whimsy, named their auto service business "Rock Springs Parts" as an offbeat tribute. Customers leave the shop reminded of Rock Springs Park thanks to the Virginia Gardens Memorial Park and the historic marker on Carolina Avenue across the street. For a lucky few, the busy scene of traffic entering and exiting the clover leaf exchange dissolves and in its place a towering wooden roller coaster appears on the hillside, followed by rattling red cars and the delighted screams of thrill-seekers sharing one last magic moment at Rock Springs Park. (Courtesy of Christian Comm.)

Visit us at
arcadiapublishing.com

· ·